# MODERN BLACK AMERICAN FICTION WRITERS

Writers of English: Lives and Works

# MODERN BLACK AMERICAN FICTION WRITERS

Edited and with an Introduction by

Harold Bloom

CHELSEA HOUSE PUBLISHERS
New York    Philadelphia

Jacket illustration: Jacob Lawrence, *The Library* (1960) (courtesy of the National Museum of Art, Washington, DC/Art Resource).

CHELSEA HOUSE PUBLISHERS

**Editorial Director** Richard Rennert
**Executive Managing Editor** Karyn Gullen Browne
**Picture Editor** Adrian G. Allen
**Copy Chief** Robin James
**Art Director** Robert Mitchell
**Manufacturing Director** Gerald Levine

Writers of English: Lives and Works

**Senior Editor** S. T. Joshi
**Senior Designer** Rae Grant

Staff for MODERN BLACK AMERICAN FICTION WRITERS

**Assistant Editor** Mary Sisson
**Research** Richard Fumosa, Robert Green
**Picture Researcher** Pat Burns

3 5 7 9 8 6 4 2

Library of Congress Cataloging-in-Publication Data

Modern Black American fiction writers / edited and with an introduction by Harold Bloom
     p. cm.—(Writers of English)
   Includes bibliographical references (p. ).
   ISBN 0-7910-2220-X.—ISBN 0-7910-2245-5 (pbk.)
  1. American fiction—Afro-American authors—History and criticism. 2. American fiction—Afro-American authors—Bio-bibliography. 3. American fiction—20th century—History and criticism. 4. American fiction—20th century—Bio-bibliography. 5. Afro-Americans in literature. I. Bloom, Harold. II. Series.
PS374.N4M63 1994
813'.509896073—dc20                                   94-5880
[B]                                                          CIP

# ⬙ Contents

# ▣ User's Guide

THIS VOLUME PROVIDES biographical, critical, and bibliographical information on the eleven most significant black American fiction writers of the middle decades of the twentieth century. Each chapter consists of three parts: a biography of the author; a selection of brief critical extracts about the author; and a bibliography of the author's published books.

The biography supplies a detailed outline of the important events in the author's life, including his or her major writings. The critical extracts are taken from a wide array of books and periodicals, from the author's lifetime to the present, and range in content from biographical to critical to historical. The extracts are arranged in chronological order by date of writing or publication, and a full bibliographical citation is provided at the end of each extract. Editorial additions or deletions are indicated within carets.

The author bibliographies list every separate publication—including books, pamphlets, broadsides, collaborations, and works edited or translated by the author—for works published in the author's lifetime; selected important posthumous publications are also listed. Titles are those of the first edition; variant titles are supplied within carets. In selected instances dates of revised editions are given where these are significant. Pseudonymous works are listed, but not the pseudonyms under which these works were published. Periodicals edited by the author are listed only when the author has written most or all of the contents. Titles enclosed in square brackets are of doubtful authenticity. All works by the author, whether in English or in other languages, have been listed; English translations of foreign-language works are not listed unless the author has done the translation.

# ◈ The Life of the Author

# Harold Bloom

NIETZSCHE, WITH EXULTANT ANGUISH, famously proclaimed that God was dead. Whatever the consequences of this for the ethical life, its ultimate literary effect certainly would have surprised the author Nietzsche. His French disciples, Foucault most prominent among them, developed the Nietzschean proclamation into the dogma that all authors, God included, were dead. The death of the author, which is no more than a Parisian trope, another metaphor for fashion's setting of skirt-lengths, is now accepted as literal truth by most of our current apostles of what should be called French Nietzsche, to distinguish it from the merely original Nietzsche. We also have French Freud or Lacan, which has little to do with the actual thought of Sigmund Freud, and even French Joyce, which interprets *Finnegans Wake* as the major work of Jacques Derrida. But all this is as nothing compared to the final triumph of the doctrine of the death of the author: French Shakespeare. That delicious absurdity is given us by the New Historicism, which blends Foucault and California fruit juice to give us the Word that Renaissance "social energies," and not William Shakespeare, composed *Hamlet* and *King Lear*. It seems a proper moment to murmur "enough" and to return to a study of the life of the author.

Sometimes it troubles me that there are so few masterpieces in the vast ocean of literary biography that stretches between James Boswell's great *Life* of Dr. Samuel Johnson and the late Richard Ellmann's wonderful *Oscar Wilde*. Literary biography is a crucial genre, and clearly a difficult one in which to excel. The actual nature of the lives of the poets seems to have little effect upon the quality of their biographies. Everything happened to Lord Byron and nothing at all to Wallace Stevens, and yet their biographers seem equally daunted by them. But even inadequate biographies of strong writers, or of weak ones, are of immense use. I have never read a literary biography from which I have not profited, a statement I cannot make about any other genre whatsoever. And when it comes to figures who are central to us—Dante, Shakespeare, Cervantes, Montaigne, Goethe, Whitman, Tolstoi, Freud, Joyce, Kafka among them—we reach out eagerly for every scrap that the biographers have gleaned. Concerning Dante and Shakespeare we know much too little, yet when we come to Goethe and Freud, where we seem to know more than everything, we still want to know more. The death of the author, despite our current resentniks, clearly was only a momentary fad. Something vital in every authentic lover of literature responds to Emerson's battle-cry sentence: "There is no history, only biography." Beyond that there is a deeper truth, difficult to come at and requiring a lifetime to understand, which is that there is no literature, only autobiography, however mediated, however veiled, however transformed. The events of Shakespeare's life included the composition of *Hamlet,* and that act of writing was itself a crucial act of living, though we do not yet know altogether how to read so doubled an act. When an author takes up a more overtly autobiographical stance, as so many do in their youth, again we still do not know precisely how to accommodate the vexed relation between life and work. T. S. Eliot, meditating upon James Joyce, made a classic statement as to such accommodation:

> We want to know who are the originals of his characters, and what were
> the origins of his episodes, so that we may unravel the web of memory
> and invention and discover how far and in what ways the crude material
> has been transformed.

When a writer is not even covertly autobiographical, the web of memory and invention is still there, but so subtly woven that we may never unravel it. And yet we want deeply never to stop trying, and not merely because we are curious, but because each of us is caught in her own network of memory and invention. We do not always recall our inventions, and long before we age we cease to be certain of the extent to which we have invented our memories. Perhaps one motive for reading is our need to unravel our own webs. If our masters could make, from their lives, what we read, then we can be moved by them to ask: What have we made or lived in relation to what we have read? The answers may be sad, or confused, but the question is likely, implicitly, to go on being asked as long as we read. In Freudian terms, we are asking: What is it that we have repressed? What have we forgotten, unconsciously but purposively: What is it that we flee? Art, literature necessarily included, is regression in the service of the ego, according to a famous Freudian formula. I doubt the Freudian wisdom here, but indubitably it is profoundly suggestive. When we read, something in us keeps asking the equivalent of the Freudian questions: From what or whom is the author in flight, and to what earlier stages in her life is she returning, and why?

Reading, whether as an art or a pastime, has been damaged by the visual media, television in particular, and might be in some danger of extinction in the age of the computer, except that the psychic need for it continues to endure, presumably because it alone can assuage a central loneliness in elitist society. Despite all sophisticated or resentful denials, the reading of imaginative literature remains a quest to overcome the isolation of the individual consciousness. We can read for information, or entertainment, or for love of the language, but in the end we seek, in the author, the person whom we have not found, whether in ourselves or in others. In that quest, there always are elements at once aggressive and defensive, so that reading, even in childhood, is rarely free of hidden anxieties. And yet it remains one of the few activities not contaminated by an entropy of spirit. We read in hope, because we lack companionship, and the author can become the object of the most idealistic elements in our search for the wit and inventiveness we so desperately require. We read biography, not as a supplement to reading the author, but as a second, fresh attempt to understand what always seems to evade us in the work, our drive towards a kind of identity with the author.

This will-to-identity, though recently much deprecated, is a prime basis for the experience of sublimity in reading. *Hamlet* retains its unique position in the Western canon not because most readers and playgoers identify themselves with the prince, who clearly is beyond them, but rather because they find themselves again in the power of the language that represents him with such immediacy and force. Yet we know that neither language nor social energy created Hamlet. Our curiosity about Shakespeare is endless, and never will be appeased. That curiosity itself is a value, and cannot be separated from the value of *Hamlet* the tragedy, or Hamlet the literary character. It provokes us that Shakespeare the man seems so unknowable, at once everyone and no one as Borges shrewdly observes. Critics keep telling us otherwise, yet something valid in us keeps believing that we would know Hamlet better if Shakespeare's life were as fully known as the lives of Goethe and Freud, Byron and Oscar Wilde, or best of all, Dr. Samuel Johnson. Shakespeare never will have his Boswell, and Dante never will have his Richard Ellmann. How much one would give for a detailed and candid *Life of Dante* by Petrarch, or an outspoken memoir of Shakespeare by Ben Jonson! Or, in the age just past, how superb would be rival studies of one another by Hemingway and Scott Fitzgerald! But the list is endless: think of *Oscar Wilde* by Lord Alfred Douglas, or a joint biography of Shelley by Mary Godwin, Emilia Viviani, and Jane Williams. More than our insatiable desire for scandal would be satisfied. The literary rivals and the lovers of the great writers possessed perspectives we will never enjoy, and without those perspectives we dwell in some poverty in regard to the writers with whom we ourselves never can be done.

There is a sense in which imaginative literature *is* perspectivism, so that the reader is likely to be overwhelmed by the work's difficulty unless its multiple perspectives are mastered. Literary biography matters most because it is a storehouse of perspectives, frequently far surpassing any that are grasped by the particular biographer. There are relations between authors' lives and their works of kinds we have yet to discover, because our analytical instruments are not yet advanced enough to perform the necessary labor. Perhaps a novel, poem, or play is not so much a regression in the service of the ego, as it is an amalgam of *all* the Freudian mechanisms of defense, all working together for the apotheosis of the ego. Freud valued art highly, but thought that the aesthetic enterprise was no rival for psycho-analysis, unlike religion and philosophy. Clearly Freud was mistaken; his own anxieties about his indebtedness to Shakespeare helped produce the weirdness of his joining in the lunacy that argued for the Earl of Oxford as the author of Shakespeare's plays. It was Shakespeare, and not "the poets," who was there before Freud arrived at his depth psychology, and it is Shakespeare who is there still, well out ahead of psychoanalysis. We see what Freud would not see, that psychoanalysis is Shakespeare prosified and systematized. Freud is part of literature, not of "science," and the biography of Freud has the same relations to psychoanalysis as the biography of Shakespeare has to *Hamlet* and *King Lear*, if only we knew more of the life of Shakespeare.

Western literature, particularly since Shakespeare, is marked by the representa-tion of internalized change in its characters. A literature of the ever-growing inner self is in itself a large form of biography, even though this is the biography of imaginary beings, from Hamlet to the sometimes nameless protagonists of Kafka and Beckett. Skeptics might want to argue that all literary biography concerns imaginary beings, since authors make themselves up, and every biographer gives us a creation curiously different from the same author as seen by the writer of a rival *Life*. Boswell's Johnson is not quite anyone else's Johnson, though it is now very difficult for us to disentangle the great Doctor from his gifted Scottish friend and follower. The life of the author is not merely a metaphor or a fiction, as is "the Death of the Author," but it always does contain metaphorical or fictive elements. Those elements are a part of the value of literary biography, but not the largest or the crucial part, which is the separation of the mask from the man or woman who hid behind it. James Joyce and Samuel Beckett, master and sometime disciple, were both of them enigmatic personalities, and their biographers have not, as yet, fully expounded the mystery of these contrasting natures. Beckett seems very nearly to have been a secular saint: personally disinterested, heroic in the French Resistance, as humane a person ever to have composed major fictions and dramas. Joyce, self-obsessed even as Beckett was preternaturally selfless, was the Milton of the twentieth century. Beckett was perhaps the least egoistic post-Joycean, post-Proustian, post-Kafkan of writers. Does that illuminate the problematical nature of his work, or does it simply constitute another problem? Whatever the cause, the question matters. The only death of the author that is other than literal, and that matters, is the fate only of weak writers. The strong, who become canonical, never die, which is what the canon truly is about. To be read forever is the Life of the Author.

# ⧉ *Introduction*

MORE THAN FORTY YEARS after its publication in July 1952, Ralph Ellison's *Invisible Man* retains its freshness and its extraordinary aesthetic distinction. Clearly it is a permanent American book, and is perhaps the most eminent novel produced in our country after the major phase of William Faulkner. Since it remains Ellison's only novel, an aware reader who returns to it can find himself or herself shadowed by a sense of loss. Though he is a remarkable essayist, Ellison seems fated to enjoy literary immortality for a solitary endeavor. And yet pragmatically this has been an American tradition; we tend to enshrine a single novel by most of our major figures. Henry James is the largest exception, and Faulkner nearest to him. Hawthorne's *The Scarlet Letter*, Melville's *Moby-Dick*, Twain's *Huckleberry Finn*, Hemingway's *The Sun Also Rises*, Fitzgerald's *The Great Gatsby* are a sequence of triumphs never again matched by their authors. A century hence, *Invisible Man* will join these works and only a few more, and new readers will be surprised to discover that Ellison never published a second novel. Since one could argue that *Invisible Man* is the principal African-American aesthetic achievement to date outside of the great procession of jazz genius that includes Armstrong, Ellington, Parker, and Bud Powell, there is a singular importance to Ellison's impasse after 1952. Can anything crucial about African-American literature be gleaned from Ellison's story-telling silence, or was the blocking agent implicit in Ellison's own stance as a novelist?

The "narrative of ascent and immersion" first traced by Robert B. Stepto in Ellison's novel was later developed by Douglas Robinson, who named it "the Jonah motif." Ellison, subtly aware of his book's link to Father Mapple's sermon on Jonah in *Moby-Dick*, explicitly invokes Jonah in the Invisible Man's Prologue. The protagonist listens to a recording of Louis Armstrong playing and singing "What Did I Do to Be So Black and Blue," and hears a music within the music. In that inner sphere he locates a preacher and congregation answering one another, with the preacher proclaiming: "It'll put you, glory, glory, Oh my Lawd, in the WHALE'S BELLY." A Jonah is a failed prophet, but he is also a survivor, and one remembers that the Book of Jonah is read aloud in the synagogue on the Day of Atonement. As the author of his own Book of Jonah, Ellison also wants his narrator's prophecy of destruction to fail. The Invisible Man is in direct descent from Melville's Ishmael, and like Ishmael he too does not desire to curse God and die. We have with us still many versions of Ras the Exhorter, and even more versions of Rinehart, reverend and numbers runner. It may be that Ellison could not get beyond *Invisible Man* because American society itself has failed to make that transition.

In naming their son Ralph Waldo Ellison, his parents shrewdly prophesied the Emersonian stance of the author of *Invisible Man*, whose protagonist finally rejects history and retreats into an underground version of Self-Reliance. The irony of that conclusion precludes our speaking either of the "failure" or the "success" of the Invisible Man. He certainly knows much more than he did at the start of his quest, and what he knows is that all of his fathers and models were false. Action has failed him, but in this serio-comic novel no social action could hope to succeed. Knowledge alone is sufficient for personal redemption only if you are a Gnostic, and the Invisible Man is too skeptical to affirm even that most negative of theologies. Redemption, individual or communal, is no longer the novel's quest. Illumination is sufficient, even though it cannot rescue anyone from our division into at least two nations. But how often can a contemporary novel take us beyond authentic illumination? Ellison, having taken us that far, has declined to transform his aesthetic splendor into either a myth of victimization or a lament for a lost common ground in our America.

—H. B.

# Maya Angelou
## b. 1928

MAYA ANGELOU was born Marguerite Johnson in St. Louis, Missouri, on April 4, 1928. Her life has been both remarkably varied and occasionally grim (she was raped at the age of eight by her mother's boyfriend), and she has won greater critical acclaim for her several autobiographical volumes than for her poetry and drama. She attended public schools in Arkansas and California, studied music privately, and studied dance with Martha Graham. In 1954–55 she was a member of the cast of *Porgy and Bess,* which went on a twenty-two-nation world tour sponsored by the U.S. Department of State. Some of her songs were recorded on the album *Miss Calypso* (1957). Later she acted in several off-Broadway plays, including one, the musical *Cabaret for Freedom* (1960), that she wrote with Godfrey Cambridge.

In addition to these artistic pursuits, Angelou held a variety of odd jobs in her late teens and early twenties, including streetcar conductor, Creole cook, nightclub waitress, prostitute, and madam. She has been married twice: first, around 1950, to a white man, Tosh Angelos (whose surname she adapted when she became a dancer), and then, from 1973 to 1981, to Paul Du Feu. She bore a son, Guy, at the age of sixteen.

When she was thirty Angelou moved to Brooklyn. There she met John Oliver Killens, James Baldwin, and other writers who encouraged her to write. While practicing her craft, however, she became involved in the civil rights movement. She met Martin Luther King, Jr., was appointed the northern coordinator of the Southern Christian Leadership Conference, and organized demonstrations at the United Nations. She fell in love with the South African freedom fighter Vusumzi Make, and they left for Egypt, where in 1961–62 Angelou worked as associate editor of the *Arab Observer,* an English-language newspaper in Cairo. She broke up with Make when he criticized her independence and lack of subservience to him.

In 1963 Angelou went to Ghana to be assistant administrator of the School of Music and Drama at the University of Ghana's Institute of African Studies. In the three years she was there she acted in several additional

1

plays, served as feature editor of the *African Review*, and was a contributor to the Ghanaian Broadcasting Corporation. Returning to the United States, she was a lecturer at the University of California at Los Angeles and has subsequently been a visiting professor or writer in residence at several other universities.

Angelou's first published book was *I Know Why the Caged Bird Sings* (1969), an autobiography of the first sixteen years of her life; a tremendous critical and popular success, it was nominated for a National Book Award and was later adapted for television. Two more autobiographical volumes appeared in the 1970s, *Gather Together in My Name* (1974) and *Singin' and Swingin' and Gettin' Merry Like Christmas* (1976), along with three volumes of poetry. While writing several more dramas, she wrote two screenplays (directing one of them and writing the musical scores for both) and several television plays (including a series of ten one-hour programs entitled *Blacks, Blues, Black*). She also continued to pursue her acting career and was nominated for a Tony Award in 1973 for her Broadway debut, *Look Away*. She was appointed a member of the American Revolution Bicentennial Council by President Gerald R. Ford in 1975.

In the 1980s Angelou solidified her reputation with two more autobiographies, *The Heart of a Woman* (1981) and *All God's Children Need Traveling Shoes* (1986), along with several more volumes of poetry. The peak of her fame was perhaps achieved when in 1993 she composed a poem, "On the Pulse of Morning," for the inauguration of President Bill Clinton. Angelou's latest prose work, *Wouldn't Take Nothing for My Journey Now*, a collection of essays and sketches, also appeared that year and, like most of its predecessors, was a best-seller.

Maya Angelou, who has received honorary degrees from Smith College, Mills College, and Lawrence University, currently resides in Sonoma, California.

# ▨ *Critical Extracts*

**MAYA ANGELOU**        There was shuffling and rustling around me, then Henry Reed was giving his valedictory address, "To Be or Not to Be." Hadn't he heard the whitefolks? We couldn't *be*, so the question was a waste of time. Henry's voice came out clear and strong. I feared to look at him. Hadn't he got the message? There was no "nobler in the mind" for the Negroes because the world didn't think we had minds, and they let us know it. "Outrageous fortune"? Now, that was a joke. ⟨. . .⟩

I had been listening and silently rebutting each sentence with my eyes closed; then there was a hush, which in an audience warns that something unplanned is happening. I looked up and saw Henry Reed, the conservative, the proper, the A student, turn his back to the audience and turn to us (the proud graduating class of 1940) and sing, nearly speaking,

> "Lift ev'ry voice and sing
> Till earth and heaven ring
> Ring with the harmonies of Liberty . . ."

It was the poem written by James Weldon Johnson. It was the music composed by J. Rosamond Johnson. It was the Negro national anthem. Out of habit we were singing it.

Our mothers and fathers stood in the dark hall and joined the hymn of encouragement. A kindergarten teacher led the small children onto the stage and the buttercups and daisies and bunny rabbits marked time and tried to follow:

> "Stony the road we trod
> Bitter the chastening rod
> Felt I the days when hope, unborn, had died.
> Yet with a steady beat
> Have not our weary feet
> Come to the place for which our fathers sighed?"

Every child I knew learned that song with his ABC's and along with "Jesus Loves Me This I Know." But I personally had never heard it before. Never heard the words, despite the thousands of times I had sung them. Never thought they had anything to do with me.

On the other hand, the words of Patrick Henry had made such an impression on me that I had been able to stretch myself tall and trembling and say, "I know not what course others may take, but as for me, give me liberty or give me death."

And now I heard, really for the first time:

> "We have come over a way that with tears
> has been watered,
> We have come, treading our path through
> the blood of the slaughtered."

While the echoes of the song shivered in the air, Henry Reed bowed his head, said, "Thank you," and returned to his place in the line. The tears that slipped down many faces were not wiped away in shame.

We are on top again. As always, again. We survived. The depths had been icy and dark, but now a bright sun spoke to our souls. I was no longer simply a member of the proud graduating class of 1940; I was a proud member of the wonderful, beautiful Negro race.

> Maya Angelou, *I Know Why the Caged Bird Sings* (New York: Random House, 1969), pp. 177–79

---

**ERNECE B. KELLY**      Miss Angelou confidently reaches back in memory to pull out the painful childhood times: when children fail to break the adult code, disastrously breaching faith and laws they know nothing of; when the very young swing easy from hysterical laughter to awful loneliness; from a hunger for heroes to the voluntary Pleasure-Pain game of wondering who their *real* parents are and how long before they take them to their authentic home.

Introducing herself as Marguerite, a "tender-hearted" child, the author allows her story to range in an extraordinary fashion along the field of human emotion. With a child's fatalism, a deep cut ushers in visions of an ignoble death. With a child's addiction to romance and melodrama, she imagines ending her life in the dirt-yard of a Mexican family—among strangers! It is as if Miss Angelou has a Time Machine, so unerringly does she record the private world of the young where sin is the Original Sin and embarrassment, penultimate. ⟨. . .⟩

Miss Angelou accommodates her literary style to the various settings her story moves through. She describes a rural vignette which is "sweet-milk fresh in her memory . . ." and a San Francisco rooming house where "Chicken suppers and gambling games were rioting on a twenty-four hour basis down-stairs." Her metaphors are strong and right; her similes less often so. But these lapses in poetic style are undeniably balanced by the insight she offers into the effects of social conditioning on the life-style and self-concept of a Black child growing up in the rural South of the 1930's.

This is a novel about Blackness, youth, and white American society, usually in conflict. The miracle is that out of the War emerges a whole person capable of believing in her worth and capabilities. On balance, it is a gentle indictment of white American womanhood. It is a timely book.

Ernece B. Kelly, [Review of *I Know Why the Caged Bird Sings*], *Harvard Educational Review* 40, No. 4 (November 1970): 681–82

**SIDONIE ANN SMITH**     Maya Angelou's autobiography, like ⟨Richard⟩ Wright's, opens with a primal childhood scene that brings into focus the nature of the imprisoning environment from which the self will seek escape. The black girl child is trapped within the cage of her own diminished self-image around which interlock the bars of natural and social forces. The oppression of natural forces, of physical appearance and processes, foists a self-consciousness on all young girls who must grow from children into women. Hair is too thin or stringy or mousy or nappy. Legs are too fat, too thin, too bony, the knees too bowed. Hips are too wide or not wide enough. Breasts grow too fast or not at all. The self-critical process is incessant, a driving demon. But in the black girl child's experience these natural bars are reinforced with the rusted iron social bars of racial subordination and impotence. Being born black is itself a liability in a world ruled by white standards of beauty which imprison the child *a priori* in a cage of ugliness: "What you looking at me for?" This really isn't me. I'm white with long blond hair and blue eyes, with pretty pink skin and straight hair, with a delicate mouth. I'll try again. The black and blue bruises of the soul multiply and compound as the caged bird flings herself against these bars:

> The Black female is assaulted in her tender years by all those common forces of nature at the same time that she is caught in the tripartite crossfire of masculine prejudice, white illogical hate and Black lack of power.

Within this imprisoning environment there is no place for this black girl child. She becomes a displaced person whose pain is intensified by her consciousness of that displacement:

> If growing up is painful for the Southern Black girl, being aware of her displacement is the rust on the razor that threatens the throat.
> It is an unnecessary insult.

If the black man is denied his potency and his masculinity, if his autobiography narrates the quest of the black male after a "place" of full manhood, the black woman is denied her beauty and her quest is one after self-accepted black womanhood. Thus the discovered pattern of significant moments Maya Angelou superimposes on the experience of her life is a pattern of moments that trace the quest of the black female after a "place," a place where a child no longer need ask self-consciously, "What you looking at me for?" but where a woman can declare confidently, "I am a beautiful, Black woman."

Sidonie Ann Smith, "The Song of a Caged Bird: Maya Angelou's Quest After Self-Acceptance," *Southern Humanities Review* 7, No. 4 (Fall 1973): 368

---

**ANNIE GOTTLIEB**     *Gather Together in My Name* is a little shorter and thinner than its predecessor; telling of an episodic, searching and wandering period in Maya Angelou's life, it lacks the density of childhood. In full compensation, her style has both ripened and simplified. It is more telegraphic and more condensed, transmitting a world of sensation or emotion or understanding in one image—in short, it is more like poetry. (Maya Angelou published a book of poems, *Just Give Me a Cool Drink of Water 'Fore I Diiie*, in between the two autobiographical volumes.)

"Disappointment rode his face bareback." "Dumbfounded, founded in dumbness." "The heavy opulence of Dostoevsky's world was where I had lived forever. The gloomy, lightless interiors, the complex ratiocinations of the characters and their burdensome humors, were as familiar to me as loneliness." "The South I returned to . . . was flesh-real and swollen belly poor." "I clenched my reason and forced their faces into focus." Even in these short bits snipped out of context, you can sense the palpability, the precision and the rhythm of this writing. ⟨. . .⟩

In *Gather Together in My Name*, the ridiculous and touching posturing of a young girl in the throes of growing up are superimposed on the serious business of survival and responsibility for a child. Maya Angelou's insistence on taking full responsibility for her own life, her frank and humorous examination of her self, will challenge many a reader to be as honest under easier circumstances. Reading her book, you may learn, too, the embrace and ritual, the dignity and solace and humor of the black community. You will meet strong, distinctive people, drawn with deftness and compassion; their blackness is not used to hide their familiar but vulnerable humanity any more than their accessible humanity can for a moment be used to obscure their blackness—or their oppression. Maya Angelou's second book about her life as a young black woman in America is engrossing and vital, rich and funny and wise.

Annie Gottlieb, "Growing Up and the Serious Business of Survival," *New York Times Book Review*, 16 June 1974, pp. 16, 20

---

**FRANK LAMONT PHILLIPS**     Maya Angelou begins the second book of her autobiography, *Gather Together in My Name*, with a brief history of Black American thought and culture after the second World War; it is not a precise history, certainly not history as viewed coolly and through statistics. It is not even "accurate," but viewed from the vantage of almost 30 years, as one might hear it on the streets: biased, authoritative, hip, almost wildly funny, like certain urban myths. It seems right, and if this is not history as it was, it is history as it should have been. ⟨. . .⟩

Maya Angelou is not the stylist that Himes is, nor a Richard Wright. She manages, however, a witty poetic flow (intensely more successful than in her book of poems, *Just Give Me a Cool Drink of Water 'Fore I Diiie*) that is sometimes cute, sometimes lax, often apt. The events of her life make interesting if somewhat lurid reading: an unwed mother, she is unlucky in love; she becomes a prostitute, enduring every nadir of fortune, her motherly instincts intact, her ability to adapt to adversity functioning.

Miss Angelou has the right instincts, that mythomania which one who is given to prattling about his life seems to possess. She applies it cannily, preserving the fiction that one can recall and, from a distance, whole conversations and surrounding trivia—as if she were a reel of recording tape, consuming for later regurgitation a problematic life. Further, she is schooled in situation ethics, licensing them retroactively to cover her having been a prostitute, making it seem almost enviable that she pulled it off so well.

It can also be said that Miss Angelou possesses an ear for folkways; they spawn abundantly in the warm stream of narration, adding enough mother wit and humor to give the events a "rightness." To some extent she is coy, never allowing us a really good, voyeur's glimpse into the conjugal bed that several male characters enjoy with her; rather, she teases. And though the author is never mawkishly sentimental, she shows herself to have been, like most of us, silly, only more so than many of us will admit. Yet she is proud. She stumbles, falls, but like the phoenix, rises renewed and wholly myth.

> Frank Lamont Phillips, [Review of *Gather Together in My Name*], *Black World* 24, No. 9 (July 1975): 52, 61

---

**ALLEN PACE NILSEN**      Last fall, Maya Angelou came out with a highly acclaimed third part of her autobiography. Entitled *Singin' and Swingin' and Gettin' Merry Like Christmas*, it does not need to be read as a continuation of the other two volumes, *I Know Why the Caged Bird Sings* and *Gather Together in My Name*, although people who have read those books will be especially interested in the new one.

Besides the always present Angelou zest and style, a value of the book is that it covers the period of her life when she made the transition from being part-time clerk in a record store to being "somebody." The part of the book that fascinated me the most was the recounting of her tour as a featured dancer in *Porgy and Bess* when it played in Italy, France, Greece, Yugoslavia, and Egypt. Because of the cast of characters, Angelou's keen sense of observation, and her lively writing, this is no ordinary travelogue. For readers who have a harder time getting into poetry than into prose, this book might make an exciting introduction to Angelou's poetry.

> Allen Pace Nilsen, "A Roundup of Good Books," *English Journal* 66, No. 6 (September 1977): 87–88

---

**SONDRA O'NEALE**      Unlike her poetry, which is a continuation of traditional oral expression in Afro-American literature, Angelou's prose follows classic technique in nonpoetic Western forms. The material in each book while chronologically marking her life is nonetheless arranged in loosely structured plot sequences which are skillfully controlled. In *Caged Bird* the tenuous psyche of a gangly, sensitive, withdrawn child is traumatically jarred by rape, a treacherous act from which neither the reader nor the protagonist has recovered by the book's end. All else is cathartic: her uncles' justified revenge upon the rapist, her years of readjustment in a closed world of speechlessness despite the warm nurturing of her grandmother, her grand-uncle, her beloved brother Bailey, and the Stamps community; a second reunion with her vivacious mother; even her absurdly unlucky pregnancy at the end does not assuage the reader's anticipatory wonder: isn't the act of rape by a trusted adult so assaultive upon an eight-year-old's life that it leaves a wound which can never be healed? Such reader interest in a character's future is the craft from which quality fiction is made. Few autobiographers however have the verve to seize the drama of such a moment, using one specific incident to control the book but with an underlining implication that the incident will not control a life.

The denouement in *Gather Together in My Name* is again sexual: the older, crafty, experienced man lasciviously preying upon the young, vulnerable, and, for all her exposure by that time, naïve woman. While foreshadowing apprehension guided the reader to the central action in the first work, Maya presses the evolvement in *Gather Together* through a limited first-person narrator who seems to know less of the villain's intention than is obvious to the reader. Thrice removed from the action, the reader sees that L. D. Tolbrook is nothing but a slick pimp, that his seductive sexual refusals can only lead to a calamitous end; that his please-turn-these-few-tricks-for-me-baby-so-I-can-get-out-of-an-urgent-jam line is an ancient inducement for susceptible females, but Maya the actor in the tragedy cannot. She is too much in love. Maya, the author, through whose eyes we see a younger, foolish "self," so painstakingly details the girl's descent into the brothel that Black women, all women, have enough vicarious example to avoid the trap. Again, through using the "self" as role model, not only is Maya able to instruct and inspire the reader but the sacrifice of personal disclosure authenticates the autobiography's integral depth.

Sondra O'Neale, "Reconstruction of the Complete Self: New Images of Black Women in Maya Angelou's Continuing Autobiography," *Black Women Writers (1950–1980): A Critical Evaluation*, ed. Mari Evans (New York: Anchor Books/Doubleday, 1984), pp. 32–33

---

**CHRISTINE FROULA**          Mr. Freeman's abuse of Maya ⟨in *I Know Why the Caged Bird Sings*⟩ occurs in two episodes. In the first, her mother rescues her from a nightmare by taking her into her own bed, and Maya then awakes to find her mother gone to work and Mr. Freeman grasping her tightly. The child feels, first, bewilderment and terror: "His right hand was moving so fast and his heart was beating so hard that I was afraid that he would die." When Mr. Freeman subsides, however, so does Maya's fright: "Finally he was quiet, and then came the nice part. He held me so softly that I wished he wouldn't ever let me go. . . . This was probably my real father and we had found each other at last." After the abuse comes the silencing: Mr. Freeman enlists the child's complicity by an act of metaphysical violence, informing her that he will kill her beloved brother Bailey if she tells anyone what "they" have done. For the child, this prohibition prevents not so much telling as asking, for, confused as she is by her conflicting feelings, she has no idea what has happened. One day, however, Mr. Freeman stops her as she is setting out for the library, and it is then that he commits the actual rape on the terrified child, "a breaking and entering when even the senses are torn apart." Again threatened with violence if she tells, Maya retreats to her bed in a silent delirium, but the story emerges when her mother discovers her stained drawers, and Mr. Freeman is duly arrested and brought to trial. ⟨. . .⟩

Maya breaks her silence when a woman befriends her by taking her home and reading aloud to her, then sending her off with a book of poems, one of which she is to recite on her next visit. We are not told which poem it was, but later we find that the pinnacle of her literary achievement at age twelve was to have learned by heart the whole of Shakespeare's *Rape of Lucrece*—nearly two thousand lines. Maya, it appears, emerges from her literal silence into a literary one. Fitting her voice to Shakespeare's words, she writes safe limits around the exclamations of her wounded tongue and in this way is able to reenter the cultural text that her words had formerly disrupted. But if Shakespeare's poem redeems Maya from her hysterical silence, it is also a lover that she embraces at her peril. In Angelou's text, Shakespeare's Lucrece represents that violation of the spirit which Shakespeare's and all stories of sleeping beauties commit upon the female reader. Maya's feat of memory signals a double seduction: by the white culture that her grandmother wished her black child not to love and by the male culture which imposes upon the rape victim, epitomized in Lucrece, the double silence of a beauty that serves male fantasy and a death that serves male honor. The black child's identification with an exquisite rape fantasy of white male culture violates her reality. Wouldn't everyone be surprised, she muses, "when one day I woke out of my black ugly dream, and my real hair, which was long and blond, would take the place of the kinky mass that Momma wouldn't let me straighten? My light-blue eyes were going to hypnotize them. . . . Because I was really white and because a cruel fairy stepmother, who was understandably jealous of my beauty, had turned me into a too-big Negro girl, with nappy black hair, broad feet, and a space between her teeth that would hold a number two pencil." Maya's fantasy bespeaks her cultural seduction, but Angelou's powerful memoir, recovering the history that frames it, rescues the child's voice from this seduction by telling the prohibited story.

> Christine Froula, "The Daughter's Seduction: Sexual Violence and Literary History,"
> *Signs* 11, No. 4 (Summer 1986): 634–37

---

**MARY JANE LUPTON**      *All God's Children Need Traveling Shoes* opens by going back in time to Angelou the mother, who anxiously waits at the hospital following Guy's car accident. In an image that parodies the well-fed mother of *The Heart of a Woman*, Angelou compares her anxiety over Guy to being eaten up:

> July and August of 1962 stretched out like fat men yawning after
> a sumptuous dinner. They had every right to gloat, for they had
> eaten me up. Gobbled me down. Consumed my spirit, not in a
> wild rush, but slowly, with the obscene patience of certain victors.
> I became a shadow walking in the white hot streets, and a dark
> spectre in the hospital.

The months of helplessly waiting for Guy to heal are like fat, stuffed men, a description that evokes memories of Reverend Thomas, who ate Momma Henderson's chicken, and of Mr. Freeman, who ate in Vivian Baxter's kitchen and raped her daughter. Guy's accident has an effect similar to the rape; Angelou retreats into silence. She is a "shadow," a "dark spectre," a Black mother silenced by the fear of her son's possible death.

Guy does recover. Their relationship, which like the autobiographical form itself is constantly in flux, moves once again from dependence to independence, climaxing in a scene in which Angelou learns that her son is having an affair with an American woman a year older than herself. Angelou at first threatens to strike him, but Guy merely pats her head and says: "Yes, little mother. I'm sure you will." Shortly afterwards Angelou travels to Germany to perform in Genet's *The Blacks*. Guy meets her return flight and takes her home to a dinner of fried chicken he has cooked for her. Then, asserting his independence, he announces that he has "plans for dinner."

Reading between the texts, we see Angelou alone again before a plate of chicken, as she was at the conclusion of *The Heart of a Woman*. In the *Traveling Shoes* episode, however, the conflicting feelings of love and resentment are more directly stated:

> He's gone. My lovely little boy is gone and will never return.
> That big confident strange man has done away with my little boy,
> and he has the gall to say he loves me. How can he love me? He
> doesn't know me, and I sure as hell don't know him.

In this passage Angelou authentically faces and records the confusions of seeing one's child achieve selfhood, universalizing the pain a mother experiences when her "boy" is transformed into a "big confident strange man" who refuses to be his mother's "beautiful appendage."

Mary Jane Lupton, "Singing the Black Mother: Maya Angelou and Autobiographical Continuity," *Black American Literature Forum* 24, No. 2 (Summer 1990): 272–73

---

**DOLLY A. McPHERSON**       Through the genre of autobiography, Angelou has celebrated the richness and vitality of Southern Black life and the sense of community that persists in the face of poverty and racial prejudice, initially revealing this celebration through a portrait of life as experienced by a Black child in the Arkansas of the 1930s (*I Know Why the Caged Bird Sings*, 1970). The second delineates a young woman struggling to create an existence that provides security and love in post–World War II America (*Gather Together in My Name*, 1974). The third presents a young, married adult in the 1950s seeking a career in show business and experiencing her first amiable contacts with Whites (*Singin' and Swingin' and Gettin' Merry Like Christmas*, 1976). The fourth volume (*The Heart of a Woman*, 1981) shows a wiser, more mature woman in the 1960s, examining the roles of being a woman and a mother. In her most recent volume, Angelou demonstrates that *All God's Children Need Traveling Shoes* (1986) to take them beyond familiar borders and to enable them to see and understand the world from another's vantage point.

While the burden of this serial autobiography is essentially a recapturing of her own subjective experiences, Angelou's effort throughout her work is to describe the influences—personal as well as cultural, historical and social—that have shaped her life. Dominant in Angelou's autobiography is the exploration of the self—the self in relationship with intimate others: the family, the community, the world. Angelou does not recount these experiences simply because they occurred, but because they represent stages of her spiritual growth and awareness—what one writer calls "stages of self." ⟨. . .⟩

A study of Maya Angelou's autobiography is significant not only because the autobiography offers insights into personal and group experience in America, but because it creates a unique place within Black autobiographical tradition, not because it is better than its formidable autobiographical predecessors, but because Angelou, throughout her autobiographical writing, adopts a special stance in relation to the self, the community and the world. Angelou's concerns with family and community, as well as with work and her conceptions of herself as a human being, are echoed throughout her autobiography. The ways in which she faces these concerns offer instruction into the range of survival strategies available to women in America and reveal, as well, important insights into Black traditions and culture.

Dolly A. McPherson, *Order out of Chaos: The Autobiographical Works of Maya Angelou*
(New York: Peter Lang, 1990), pp. 5–6

---

**CAROL E. NEUBAUER**        From time to time, Angelou sees marriage as the answer to her own sense of dislocation and fully envisions a perfect future with various prospective husbands. While in New York, she meets Vusumzi Make, a black South African freedom fighter, and imagines that he will provide her with the same domestic security she had hoped would develop from other relationships: "I was getting a husband, and a part of that gift was having someone to share responsibility and guilt." Yet her hopes are even more idealistic than usual, inasmuch as she imagines herself participating in the liberation of South Africa as Vus Make's wife: "With my courage added to his own, he would succeed in bringing the ignominious white rule in South Africa to an end. If I didn't already have the qualities he needed, then I would develop them. Infatuation made me believe in my ability to create myself into my lover's desire." In reality, Angelou is only willing to go so far in re-creating herself to meet her husband's desires and is all too soon frustrated with her role as Make's wife. He does not want her to work but is unable on his own to support his expensive tastes as well as his family. They are evicted from their New York apartment just before they leave for Egypt and soon face similar problems in Cairo. Their marriage dissolves after some months, despite Angelou's efforts to contribute to their financial assets by working as editor of the *Arab Observer*. In *Heart of a Woman*, she underscores the illusory nature of her fantasy about marriage to show how her perspective has shifted over the years and how much understanding she has gained about life in general. Re-creating these fantasies in her autobiography is a subtle form of truth telling and a way to present hard-earned insights about her life to her readers.

Carol E. Neubauer, "Maya Angelou: Self and a Song of Freedom in the Southern Tradition," *Southern Women Writers: The New Generation*, ed. Tonette Bond Inge (Tuscaloosa: University of Alabama Press, 1990), pp. 127–28

---

**ROBERT FULGHUM**    After five volumes of autobiography and five volumes of poetry, Maya Angelou offers us this very small volume of 24 poetically entitled essays so carefully crafted they cover only 54 actual pages of writing. Her publisher, Random House, has assigned the book to the publishing category "Inspiration/Self-Help." But *Wouldn't Take Nothing for My Journey Now* really belongs in an even more prestigious location in a bookstore, labeled "Wisdom Literature." ⟨. . .⟩

Angelou has dedicated this book to Oprah Winfrey. Not a casual gesture, it is a salute to the speaker at the head table of the banquet of sisterhood.

Maya Angelou has, of course, become one of these wise women herself, as her new book so clearly demonstrates. At the end of the first essay, she writes: "Women should be tough, tender, laugh as much as possible, and live long lives. The struggle for equality continues unabated, and the woman warrior who is armed with wit and courage will be among the first to celebrate victory." As of this past January, millions of Americans realize how certainly this celebration is underway. ⟨. . .⟩

To read these essays carefully, slowly, even one a day over a month, is to feel you are there with Maya Angelou on her day away, leaning back in the shade of an old tree on a hot afternoon; after an arduous journey you have come home. The companion who has waited for you is older than you are. She knows where you've been. Like the prodigal son, she too has wandered in foreign lands and returned again and again to the place where she began. She has known pain and sorrow, sinfulness and saintliness. Yet she can sing and dance, recite poems, speak with words of silence and make you laugh or cry. There is no finer company than hers. She has something to tell you now. Listen. She is wise.

> Robert Fulghum, "Home Truths and Homilies," *Washington Post Book World*, 19 September 1993, p. 4

# ◈ *Bibliography*

*I Know Why the Caged Bird Sings*. 1969.

*Just Give Me a Cool Drink of Water 'Fore I Diiie: The Poetry of Maya Angelou*. 1971, 1988 (with *Oh Pray My Wings Are Gonna Fit Me Well*).

*Gather Together in My Name*. 1974, 1985.

*Oh Pray My Wings Are Gonna Fit Me Well*. 1975.

*Singin' and Swingin' and Gettin' Merry Like Christmas*. 1976.

*And Still I Rise*. 1978.

*Weekend Glory*. 198-.

*The Heart of a Woman*. 1981.

*Poems*. 1981, 1986.

*Shaker, Why Don't You Sing?* 1983.

*All God's Children Need Traveling Shoes*. 1986.

*Now Sheba Sings the Songs*. 1986.

*Conversations with Maya Angelou*. Ed. Jeffrey M. Elliot. 1989.

*I Shall Not Be Moved*. 1990.

*Maya Angelou Omnibus*. 1991.

*On the Pulse of Morning*. 1993.

*Soul Looks Back in Wonder*. 1993.

*Lessons in Living*. 1993.

*Life Doesn't Frighten Me*. 1993.

*Wouldn't Take Nothing for My Journey Now*. 1993.

*I Love the Look of Words*. 1993.

*And My Best Friend Is Chicken*. 1994.

# William Attaway
## *1911–1986*

WILLIAM ALEXANDER ATTAWAY was born on November 19, 1911, in Green-
ville, Mississippi, to William A. and Florence Parry Attaway. Attaway's
father was a physician who in 1921 helped to found the National Negro
Insurance Association; he also moved his family to Chicago to escape the
pervasive racism of the South, part of the "Great Migration" about which
his son would later write.

Attaway rebelled against the bourgeois lifestyle of his educated and financially secure parents, opting to attend a vocational rather than an academic
high school. He finally bowed to his parents' wishes and entered the University of Illinois, but after his father's death he dropped out for two years and
lived as a vagabond, working as a seaman, dockworker, and salesman before
finally returning to the University of Illinois and earning a B.A. in 1936.
He had decided to become a writer after reading the work of Langston
Hughes in high school. In 1935 Attaway was briefly associated with the
Federal Writers' Project of the Work Projects Administration, where he
met Richard Wright; in that year he produced a play, *Carnival*, for his
sister's amateur dramatic group.

After graduation Attaway moved to New York, where he wrote his first
novel, *Let Me Breathe Thunder* (1939), whose rugged naturalism was probably
inspired by John Steinbeck's *Of Mice and Men*. Although the two main
characters are white, Attaway drew upon his own hobo experiences in this
novel of vagabonds befriending a young Mexican boy as they travel across
the country.

In 1939 Attaway received a two-year grant from the Rosenwald Foundation, allowing him to produce his second novel, *Blood on the Forge* (1941).
This work has been praised by critics as an important study of the Great
Migration, chronicling the hardships of three black brothers who travel
from rural Kentucky to a steel mill in the Allegheny Valley of Pennsylvania.
Here Attaway combines racial and proletarian themes in an indictment of
industrialism.

Although both of Attaway's novels were critically well received, neither of them sold very well, and he turned to more profitable pursuits. He wrote a collection of songs, *Calypso Song Book* (1957), and a history of popular music for children, *Hear America Singing* (1967). He also wrote songs for his friend Harry Belafonte as well as scripts for radio, television, and film. Some of his media work addressed racial issues, such as his television script on black humor, *One Hundred Years of Laughter* (1966). In 1968 he wrote several drafts of a screenplay of the film adaptation of Irving Wallace's novel *The Man*, about a black man who becomes president of the United States, but his work was found unsuitable and was not used in the final version.

Attaway married Frances Settele on December 28, 1962; they had two children. He and his family moved to Barbados in 1966, remaining there for eleven years before moving to California. William Attaway died in Los Angeles on June 17, 1986.

# ▧ *Critical Extracts*

**ULYSSES LEE**     It would be unfortunate if Mr. Attaway's book ⟨*Let Me Breathe Thunder*⟩ should come to be known, in the words of the jacket blurb and the brief prefatory note, as "that rare thing, a novel by a Negro about whites." For the novel—it is really a long story and not a novel at all—can very well stand on its own feet as a thoroughly readable tale of disinherited youth on the road; it needs no novelty publicity. Moreover, it is no more a novel of whites than it is one of Negroes. Mag and Cooper, colored owners of a string of houses of prostitution in Yakima, Washington, are among the best-realized characters in the book. ⟨. . .⟩

The most striking feature of the novel, however, is not Mr. Attaway's choice of whites as his central characters; it is his choice of a phase of the American youth problem that is too little known to the novel-reading public. When he turns to a novel primarily of Negro life, he should produce one which will do much for Negro literature, at present bound closely to the cities and selected Southern areas, all too purposefully portraying a Negro "of whom we can be proud" rather than one whom we can recognize.

Ulysses Lee, "On the Road," *Opportunity* 17, No. 9 (September 1939): 283–84

**DRAKE DE KAY**      Written by a Negro author with notable objectivity, this ⟨*Blood on the Forge*⟩ is a starkly realistic story involving social criticism as searching as any to be found in contemporary literature; but Mr. Attaway, though his protagonists are of his own race, has not singled out the Negro as the sole victim of unjust conditions. He shows native white Americans and immigrant Slavs working under the same system of low pay, cruelly long hours and unnecessary hazards to life and limb. Many of these injustices have since been rectified, but that fact does not detract from the story value of a tale which holds one's attention, primarily by its realistic characterizations, the vividness and intensity of dramatic moments and its pathos. There is a double theme: the Negro competing with the white man in an abnormal condition of the labor market; and the man of the soil forced to make an adjustment with urban industrial life. ⟨. . .⟩

This novel portraying life in the raw is not for those who shun the unlovely aspects of human nature, who have a distaste for bloodshed and the cruder manifestations of sex. Indeed one of its chief claims to literary distinction consists in its author's refusal to sentimentalize his earthy men and women. The artistic integrity Mr. Attaway evinced in his first book, *Let Me Breathe Thunder*, is equally evident in the faithful depiction of the primitive approach to life of a social group on whose laborious efforts the whole scheme of modern industrial life is based.

> Drake De Kay, "The Color Line," *New York Times Book Review*, 24 August 1941, pp. 18, 20

---

**RALPH ELLISON**      The contribution of *Blood on the Forge* lies in its projection of new themes. Spanning two areas and two eras of Negro experience, those of the semi-feudal plantation and the industrial urban environments, Attaway's source material receives its dynamic movement from the clash of two modes of economic production. The characters are caught in the force of a struggle which, like the steel furnaces, roars throughout its pages; they are swept out of the center of gravity of one world, blindly into that of another. (This was an experience through which the Negro acquired the consciousness out of which he acts today.) But when we examine the conclusion of the novel to see how the struggle has registered in the consciousness of Attaway's characters, we are disappointed. We find Big Mat dead, Chinatown blind, and Melody no more understanding the forces which grip him than when he first encountered them. One gets the impression that the book is simply a lament for the dying away of the Negro's folk values. The author seems to sanction the conclusions of the crippled character who, wandering in and out of the novel as a symbol of fate, keeps insisting that "It's wrong to tear up the ground and melt it up in the furnace . . . ground don't like it." But this explanation of the Negro's degradation and suffering when he enters industry is that of a pre-industrial toiler viewing a complex, mechanical world which he cannot understand. Such a viewpoint includes only part of the contradictory experience from which the novel is composed. For of the thousands of Negroes who passed through the trauma of industrialization, all were not left uprooted and brutalized, and what happened to those who were not is a necessary part of the story. This omission, aside from accounting for the artistic failures of the novel: its episodic character; its substitution of tagging (Melody, Chinatown, Big Mat) for character development, leaves unclarified an experience, the understanding of which is all important to Negroes who because of the war are faced with a future charged with doubt. The power of *Blood on the Forge* lies not so much in Attaway's presentation as in the tremendous vitality—now emphasized by the war—of the book's basic situation. There is no center of consciousness, lodged in a character or characters, capable of comprehending the sequence of events. This, possibly, would have called for an entirely new character. But at the same time it would have saved the work from finally disintegrating into a catalogue of meaningless casualties and despairs. Inclusion of such a consciousness would not have been a mere artistic device; it would have been in keeping with artistic truth.

Ralph Ellison, "Transition," *Negro Quarterly* 1, No. 1 (Spring 1942): 89–90

---

**HUGH M. GLOSTER**      William Attaway's *Let Me Breathe Thunder* (1939), which shows the influence of John Steinbeck, is primarily concerned with the experiences of Step and Ed, white boys whose outlook upon life has been hardened by underprivileged childhood and precarious vagrancy, and of Hi Boy, a spirited ten-year-old Mexican youngster. The action begins with the arrival of the trio in Seattle, where Step has a fight with the bouncer of an underground dive. Fearing vengeance, the transients board a Northern Pacific passenger train for the wheat lands of Kansas and meet Sampson, a Yakima Valley farmer, who persuades them to accept employment on his farm. Step at once deflowers Anna, Sampson's daughter, and establishes a rendezvous with her at a Yakima house of ill repute maintained by Mag, a colored prostitute. When the migrants finish their work on the farm, Anna arranges a final meeting with Step at Mag's place and is there attacked by Cooper, the Negro woman's "sweet man." In an attempt to shoot her unfaithful lover, Mag inflicts an arm wound upon Anna, who fanatically rushes into the street and exposes Step as well as Cooper. Fearing Sampson's reaction, the wanderers catch a Northern Pacific freight and on the next morning find Cooper in the same box car with them. Step wants to throw Cooper from the train, but Ed insists that the Negro be given an opportunity to explain his motives. After Cooper says that he only intended to make Mag jealous, Step relents his fury but demands that the Negro get off at the next stop. As the train moves toward the Montana Rockies, Hi Boy suffers from an infection earlier received when he plunged a fork into his hand to prove his strength and fortitude. After almost freezing in the sleet, the itinerants change to a train en route to Denver, but Hi Boy dies before medical aid can be procured.

In *Let Me Breathe Thunder* references to Negroes and racial issues are merely incidental. Nevertheless, among the best realized characters in the book are Mag, Cooper, and Black Face, the last-named being a hobo found by the travelers on a freight during the final lap of their journey to Yakima. The chief merit of the book is its realistic treatment of one of the aspects of the American youth problem. Step and Ed, warped personalities without benefit of home and school background, are doomed even before young manhood to the irregular and unstable life of those who are without settled habitation. Hi Boy, who escaped to join Step and Ed after a Mexican family with whom he was traveling was thrown from a train and arrested for burglary, is probably prevented by early death from acquiring the distorted social perspective of an indurate vagrant. Attaway does not undertake to offer a remedy for the maladjustment which he discloses; he simply describes life as he sees it.

Hugh M. Gloster, *Negro Voices in American Fiction* (Chapel Hill: University of North Carolina Press, 1948), pp. 249–50

---

**CARL MILTON HUGHES**        William Attaway's *Blood on the Forge* anticipates *Lonely Crusade* and *If He Hollers Let Him Go* by Chester Himes in the naturalistic thesis presented and in many ways so does Carl Offord's *The White Face*. The thesis in *Blood on the Forge* is that Negroes are objects of discrimination and injustice on the labor market, especially when they offer "competition to white men." Attaway develops this thesis around economic conditions in the steel mills of Pennsylvania after World War I when Negroes were brought from the South for scab labor purposes.

The plot outline is simple but filled with many possibilities of which Attaway takes full advantage. The opening scene of *Blood on the Forge* is a sharecropping farm from Kentucky. The world that Attaway creates and the shanty which he describes make the Lesters of *Tobacco Road* by Erskine Caldwell appear occupants of a hospitable and comfortable home by comparison. The principal characters, Big Matt, Chinatown, Melody, and Big Matt's wife, endure poverty and squalor in a miserable shanty. This family belongs to the class of substandard workers comparable with those under feudalism during the Middle Ages. Under such a system the human personality of the Negro workers is ignored completely. Here in an elemental existence, the three brothers live together. Despite the impoverished condition of the farm, the men are healthy and strong. Big Matt, leader of the trio, is a powerfully developed, huge, black man. Chinatown, smaller in stature but equally well-built, is slightly larger than the musically talented Melody. These three brothers share a deep-rooted attachment for each other. This affection is born from mutual understanding and common suffering. Each has a different expression for the same frustration which is self-realization as a human being. Big Matt wants to preach and holds the primordial theory of having a boy child as the only means of self-perpetuation. He daydreams of preaching, reading his Bible in his spare time. He approaches the mystic's world while Chinatown wants the brightness of this world to come into his being. Taking his cue from the sun, he has a gold tooth which is his one prized possession. Melody plays haunting strains on his guitar. Thus, these sharecropper dreamers in their private worlds present dissatisfied men who want to escape from their present life. Externally, however, they exhibit a solid demeanor which sustains them.

Modern tragedy takes into account the failures and frustrations of the life of the ordinary man in highly industrialized civilization. The machine robs man of that sense of immanence that he had in less highly developed epochs. *Blood on the Forge* shows little man meeting and experiencing tragedy in an industrialized setting. Human beings in society need not suffer such defeats and frustrations. But what should be, rarely if ever, is in accord with what is.

Carl Milton Hughes, *The Negro Novelist: A Discussion of the Writings of American Negro Novelists 1940–1950* (New York: Citadel Press, 1953), pp. 79–81, 83

**EDWARD MARGOLIES**        Attaway prepared the way for *Blood on the Forge* with *Let Me Breathe Thunder*, a novel he published two years earlier in 1939. In one sense Attaway is less inhibited in his first book because he is writing primarily about white characters whose point of view would not be readily understood as racial. Yet his protagonists, hobo migrant farm workers, are Negroes under the skin—pariahs, consumed at the same time with wanderlust and the desire to stay put. Their agony is a Negro agony, and their allusions to race problems are more "inside" than Attaway might have cared to admit. They speak on more than one occasion of interracial sex and its conspiratorial acceptance in middle-class communities, of the various kinds of racial prejudice they meet throughout the country—and the fact that only hoboes do not appear to discriminate; of the private humiliations "outsiders" experience in a bourgeois milieu, and above all of their uneasiness in accommodating themselves to the patterns of American life, and their desire not to do so. They are the alienated, the uncommitted, whose discontents may one day be marshaled toward revolution—but not necessarily of the doctrinaire, ideological variety. They do not yet know what they want, but they know what they dislike. Once they are aware of what they seek, they are perhaps capable of changing their world.

   Attaway here does not understand his people. His solution, like Toomer's, is a return to the soil. A character named Sampson, who owns orchards and farm lands, has suffered considerably during his life; his wife and sons have died and he lives alone with an adolescent daughter. But his strong sense of identification with the land serves to renew him and give him perspective and emotional balance. Sampson is portrayed most sympathetically, but Attaway cannot make him ring altogether true. And the hoboes whom he asks to stay with him on the land cannot believe in him either; as the novel closes, they leave to try their luck elsewhere. Attaway's inability to make Sampson believable stems as much from anachronism as from failure of craftsmanship. The American dream of the independent farmer was outmoded by the Depression years, and Attaway was simply unable to cope with his nostalgia.

Edward Margolies, "Migration: William Attaway's *Blood on the Forge*," *Native Sons: A Critical Study of Twentieth-Century Negro American Authors* (Philadelphia: J. B. Lippincott Co., 1968), pp. 50–51

**ROBERT FELGAR**     So much emphasis has been placed recently on nominating the important new Black novelists that attending to important older ones has been neglected. Large critical claims have been made lately for Ishmael Reed, William Melvin Kelly, and John A. Williams, while the work of William Attaway and Zora Neale Hurston, for instance, remains buried under the weight of years of critical indifference. I want to make a plea for William Attaway as a novelist, one who, like so many Afro-American writers of fiction, wrote one or two good books, and then, as in the case of Toomer, apparently was discouraged from fulfilling early promise. Attaway published his first book, *Let Me Breathe Thunder*, in 1939, his second, *Blood on the Forge*, two years later. The two are almost completely unknown by Black and white readers; both audiences should give themselves the chance to become seriously concerned with Attaway's vision.

In neither book does he embrace a prescriptive racial esthetic: many of the major characters in *Let Me Breathe Thunder* are white, in *Blood on the Forge* Black. He writes about people who engage his sympathy and imagination; sometimes they are Afro-American, sometimes white Americans. Since the implied audience for both books is "the common reader," Attaway is not confined to writing "only" about Blacks or "only" about whites. Neither color is a limitation on his writing; they are given material. The false dichotomy between "race" novels and novels of "universal significance" is fortunately not a problem for him.

The central characters in *Let Me Breathe Thunder* are estranged from bourgeois American society because although racially acceptable, they are hoboes, and therefore outsiders in social, if not racial status. As proletarians, both their stake and their place in America are problematic. They have no permanent home, employment, or social relations. Movement is the permanent ontological fact of their existence. The narrator, Ed, has perhaps a more common-sensical hold on experience than his fellow hobo, Step (using names descriptively is sustained in the later novel), but the lack of any lasting orientation in both their lives is equal. They befriend a nine-year-old Mexican youth who is even less at home in the universe than they are: Hi Boy is without parents (Step "adopts" him as Sampson becomes the temporary "father" of the two transients), without friends except Step and Ed, and without a language to articulate his plight—he has the slipperiest of grasps on English. An emblem of almost total exclusion, he dies of an infection caused by a wound in his hand he inflicted with a fork in order to prove to Step that he was not a coward. The world he greeted with his name allowed him the briefest existence only. The themes of separation and dislocation inform *Blood on the Forge* in a different way because the Moss brothers are racial as well as social outcasts.

> Robert Felgar, "William Attaway's Unaccomodated Protagonists," *Studies in Black Literature* 4, No. 1 (Spring 1973): 1

**ADDISON GAYLE, JR.**      *Blood on the Forge* is a well-written novel. It deserved the plaudits of critics past and present. It is a structurally sounder novel than *Native Son,* and the inner mechanics—symbols and images of life, death, and destruction—work as effectively for Attaway as they do for Wright. Yet, Attaway, unlike Wright, has accepted the argument that themes of universal import take preference over those of more parochial import; that is, the conflict between man and the machine is more universal than that between black man and a racist society. Under the influence of this argument, despite the coming years of the Hitler madness, the continuing brutalization of Blacks by whites, the incarceration of Japanese citizens by Americans, and the struggle of the darker peoples of the world against white colonialism, Attaway wants to deny universality to the most universal phenomenon in world history. Moreover, he wants to make Big Mat, Chinatown, and Melody into more fully developed images of the vagabonds, Step and Ed, men in conflict with a hostile environment forced to find new modes of living, yet unable to do so.

This despite the fact that Attaway lives in a universe marred by turmoil and dissension. The depression, as he knows so well, has brought men to the brink of revolution, the migration made it impossible for people to survive by the patterns of old. In such a world, Melody and Chinatown, of course, are doomed; hedonism and paganism, twin evils for black men, are useless in a world in which the race war is an eternal given. This is not so for Big Mat; in a world of violence and turmoil, violence is the norm, and the man who tempers it with the proper humanism has come close to constructing a new ethic. Attaway could not accept this idea. There is too much of the naturalist in him, too much of the sociologist; he adheres to a code that preaches universal brotherhood, yet one that refuses to acknowledge the historical fact that such has been achieved only when one man possessed guns as powerful as the other. When Big Mat exchanges the Bible for the sheriff's cudgel, he has leaped across centuries of black history into the modern world. Attaway, however, cannot accept him, recoils in horror from his own creation, attempts to convince the reader that excessive rage and compulsive anger have driven Mat to become more insane than other men, that violence represents not redemption for him, but vengeance, and that the race war, unlike other wars, must be fought out on the high plane of moral niceties and meaningless epithets. "At the moment," noted Wright, "when a people begin to realize a meaning in their suffering, the civilization that engenders that suffering is doomed."

Addison Gayle, Jr., *The Way of the New World: The Black Novel in America* (Garden City, NY: Anchor Press/Doubleday, 1975), pp. 164–65

---

**BONNIE J. BARTHOLD**        Images of barrenness ⟨in *Blood on the Forge*⟩ figure as another form of fragmentation, of human beings cut off from time and cyclic continuity. In Part I, most of Mat's farmland is so lacking in topsoil that it is barren; and he has no mule for plowing. His wife, Hattie, is barren, having suffered six or seven miscarriages. Though Anna finds in Big Mat a fulfillment of her yearning for a man "with a pine tree on his belly, hard like rock all night," by the end of Part IV she has turned to a "piece of ice" beneath him, "a dead body," and the image again is one of barrenness. Earlier, Mat has explained his barrenness as the result of a curse by God on "a child of sin." He knows how to lift the curse: "I got to preach the gospel—that the only way." But his knowledge, too, is barren: "No matter how much inside [him]," he can't preach. "If I tries to preach 'fore folks it all jest hits against the stopper in my throat and build up and build up till I fit to bust with wild words that ain't comin' out." He lacks the words to bring forth the Word, and belief is fragmented from its expression.

These various images of fragmentation are epitomized in the character of Smothers, the mad, crippled timekeeper at the mill. Smothers feels that the earth will sooner or later take revenge against the steel mill's violation of its sacredness, and the revenge will focus on the men who work the mill. "Steel gonna git you," he says. Crippled by an accident that he brought on himself as an act of defiance of the "monster" mill, he has become a kind of mill worker everyman, his crippled legs his wounds in an ongoing battle. Before he is killed, in the same explosion that takes Chinatown's eyes, his foreman has jokingly promised him that if steel "gits" him, "we make you up into watch fobs. The boys 'round the bunkhouse 'll wear you across their chests for luck." After Smothers's death, Melody passes through the bunkhouse and finds Bo keeping the promise, affixing watch chains to shreds of steel from the explosion.

Bonnie J. Barthold, "William Attaway, *Blood on the Forge*," *Black Time: Fiction of Africa, the Caribbean, and the United States* (New Haven: Yale University Press, 1981), pp. 167–68

**CYNTHIA HAMILTON**      For Attaway's character Mat ⟨in *Blood on the Forge*⟩, the mill becomes an adversary, a challenge to overcome. His strength and size are pitted against steel, and it is to prove his manhood that he returns daily. But his brother Melody finds no meaning in the work, and his fingers can no longer find their way on his guitar strings: "Here at the mill it felt right to find quick chords with the fingers—a strange kind of playing for him, but it was right for that new place." For the third brother, Chinatown, the fear of the first encounter with steel remains, as he joins the others, reluctantly, on his shift. Ironically, it is Chinatown whom "steel" identifies as defenseless when it lashes out and blinds him in a furnace explosion which kills twelve men. Known as the joy of the crowd, Chinatown seemed to smile constantly; his habit of narrowing his eyes like those of a Chinaman earned him his nickname. The steel mill takes from him the one thing from the past which assured his identity, his eyes: "He had been a man who lived through outward symbols. Now those symbols were gone, and he was lost." Maybe Melody had been right; maybe " 'the Judgment [was] jest a steel mill.' "

Attaway's portrayal of the three brothers presents symbolically what may have been the three primary consequences of urban acculturation. Mat destroys himself while trying to adjust to the new environment, using the only tools he has, those of the past. Chinatown, in fear and rejection, really never attempts to participate in the new environment; he goes to his shift at the mill, rarely works, but still cannot escape its oppression. With Melody we sense that Attaway is presenting the painful process of transformation. Though the urban industrial setting is just as alienating for Melody as it is for his brothers, he tries to adapt some of the old values and effect transformation. For example, his rural Southern music becomes the blues in the urban North, and while others are taking sides on a strike, Melody decides to stay home with his blind brother, familial obligation taking precedence over political conflict. In the end we feel that Melody will adjust to the city, but on his own terms, taking his brother and his music with him wherever he goes.

Cynthia Hamilton, "Work and Culture: The Evolution of Consciousness in Urban Industrial Society in the Fiction of William Attaway and Peter Abrahams," *Black American Literature Forum* 21, Nos. 1 & 2 (Spring–Summer 1987): 155–56

---

**SAMUEL B. GARREN**      One element of black folk culture that plays an important part in William Attaway's novel *Blood on the Forge* (1941) is the wishing game. Early in Part I, Melody, one of three Moss brothers subsisting on a poor Kentucky farm in 1919, begins the game. His motive is distraction from hunger while awaiting Big Mat, the brother who sharecrops the farm and who may bring some food. In the call-and-response fashion characteristic of Afro-American culture, Melody involves his brother Chinatown in the game: " 'China,' he half sang, 'you know where I wish I was at now?' " Chinatown needs no prodding because the brothers have often played this game, their wishes usually formed by the "grand places pictured in the old newspapers" lining the walls of their shack. Led on by the responses of Chinatown, Melody spins his narrative. He imagines himself in town on a Saturday noon, all dressed up in a "white-checkered vest and a ice-cream suit," with a gold watch chain and "yeller shoes with dimes in the toes. Man, man!"

A small detail in this apparently insignificant game reveals an important difference between Melody and the other Moss brothers. In helping along the story, Chinatown tries to add girls, but Melody says that the girls can wait until evening. Noon is the time instead for playing pool. When Chinatown objects that Melody in actuality cannot play pool, Melody replies, "But I wish I can." Unlike the other major characters in the novel,

Melody can maintain the distinction between unrealizable desires and reality. With one exception, which he quickly recognizes, Melody keeps wishing within the confines of play, part of a necessary game that the mind must perform when a person is denied opportunities and privileges by society. For others in the novel, however, the wish becomes the delusion, to be paid for with pain and even death.

Samuel B. Garren, "Playing the Wishing Game: Folkloric Elements in William Attaway's *Blood on the Forge*," *CLA Journal* 32, No. 1 (September 1988): 10–11

# Bibliography

*Let Me Breathe Thunder*. 1939.

*Blood on the Forge*. 1941.

*Calypso Song Book*. Ed. Lyle Kenyon Engel. 1957.

*Hear America Singing*. 1967.

# James Baldwin
## 1924–1987

JAMES ARTHUR BALDWIN was born on August 2, 1924, in Harlem, New York City, to Emma Berdis Jones and an unknown father. When James was three years old his mother married David Baldwin, the son of a slave, who was a factory worker and lay preacher; the couple would subsequently have eight children. Baldwin joined the Church of Mount Calvary of the Pentecostal Faith in 1938 and became a preacher, although in later years he expressed scorn and regret over his youthful religious activities. He attended De Witt Clinton High School, a largely white school in the Bronx, from 1938 to 1942. After working at a series of menial jobs in New Jersey, he moved to Greenwich Village in 1944 in order to support his family after the death of his stepfather the previous year. He met Richard Wright, whose writing exerted considerable influence on him. Failing in the attempt to write a novel, he began writing reviews in the *Nation* and the *New Leader* and gained notoriety by a controversial essay, "The Harlem Ghetto: Winter 1948," in *Commentary* for February 1948.

Later that year Baldwin won a Rosenwald Foundation Fellowship; in November he used much of the grant money to emigrate to Paris, where he remained for the next nine years, although returning frequently to New York. He associated with many of the American expatriates in Paris—Saul Bellow, Truman Capote, Herbert Gold—along with Jean-Paul Sartre, Jean Genet, and other French writers. One friend, the painter Lucien Happersberger, invited Baldwin to spend time at his home in Switzerland in 1951, where Baldwin completed his most highly regarded novel, *Go Tell It on the Mountain* (1953). This novel, drawing upon his childhood experiences, deals with the religious and social maturation of a boy in a repressive and racist society.

A Guggenheim Fellowship awarded in 1954 allowed Baldwin the leisure to work on his next book, *Giovanni's Room* (1956). This is one of the first modern novels to deal frankly with homosexuality. *Another Country* (1962), a novel on which Baldwin worked for six years, is a wide-ranging treatment of homosexual, bisexual, and interracial love; it was a tremendous popular success. He also published two noted collections of essays, *Notes of a Native Son* (1955) and *Nobody Knows My Name* (1961). Returning to the United States in 1957, Baldwin became actively involved in the civil rights movement, meeting with Martin Luther King, Jr., and becoming spokesman for the Congress on Racial Equality (CORE) and the Student Nonviolent Coordinating Committee (SNCC).

In 1963 Baldwin published the controversial *The Fire Next Time*, a collection of two essays that predict social apocalypse in America if the question of racial harmony is not addressed. The play *Blues for Mr. Charlie* (1964), a violent depiction of racism in the South, also provoked outrage from white critics. *No Name in the Street* (1972) is a still more unrestrained exposé of American racism. Nevertheless, Baldwin was labeled an "Uncle Tom" by Eldridge Cleaver in *Soul on Ice* (1968) for his lack of support of African nationalism.

Later works by Baldwin display a more subdued approach to racial issues. Such nonfictional works as *The Devil Finds Work* (1976) and *The Evidence of Things Not Seen* (1985) sensitively and complexly explore the history of race relations in the United States. Baldwin's later novels—*Tell Me How Long the Train's Been Gone* (1968), *If Beale Street Could Talk* (1974), *Little Man, Little Man* (1976), and *Just Above My Head* (1979)—combine autobiography with intricacy of character portrayal; but some critics feel that they merely repeat themes and motifs expressed better in his earlier works.

James Baldwin died of stomach cancer in St. Paul de Vence, France, on December 1, 1987.

# ▨ *Critical Extracts*

**LANGSTON HUGHES**      I think that one definition of the great artist might be the creator who projects the biggest dream in terms of the least person. There is something in Cervantes or Shakespeare, Beethoven or Rembrandt or Louis Armstrong that millions can understand. The American native son who signs his name James Baldwin is quite a ways off from fitting such a definition of a great artist in writing, but he is not as far off as many another writer who deals in picture captions or journalese in the hope of capturing and retaining a wide public. James Baldwin writes down to nobody, and he is thought-provoking, tantalizing, irritating, abusing and amusing. And he uses words as the sea uses waves, to flow and beat, advance and retreat, rise and take a bow in disappearing. ⟨. . .⟩

Few American writers handle words more effectively in the essay form than James Baldwin. To my way of thinking, he is much better at provoking thought in the essay than he is in arousing emotion in fiction. I much prefer *Notes of a Native Son* to his novel, *Go Tell It on the Mountain*, where the surface excellence and poetry of his writing did not seem to me to suit the earthiness of his subject matter. In his essays, words and material suit each other. The thought becomes poetry, and the poetry illuminates the thought.

> Langston Hughes, "From Harlem to Paris," *New York Times Book Review*, 26 February 1956, p. 26

---

**ROBERT BONE**     The best of Baldwin's novels is *Go Tell It on the Mountain* (1953), and his best is very good indeed. It ranks with Jean Toomer's *Cane*, Richard Wright's *Native Son*, and Ralph Ellison's *Invisible Man* as a major contribution to American fiction. For this novel cuts through the walls of the store-front church to the essence of Negro experience in America. This is Baldwin's earliest world, his bright and morning star, and it glows with metaphorical intensity. Its emotions are his emotions; its language, his native tongue. The result is a prose of unusual power and authority. One senses in Baldwin's first novel a confidence, control, and mastery of style that he has not attained again in the novel form.

The central event of *Go Tell It on the Mountain* is the religious conversion of an adolescent boy. In a long autobiographical essay, which forms a part of *The Fire Next Time*, Baldwin leaves no doubt that he was writing of his own experience. During the summer of his fourteenth year, he tells us, he succumbed to the spiritual seduction of a woman evangelist. On the night of his conversion, he suddenly found himself lying on the floor before the altar. He describes his trancelike state, the singing and clapping of the saints, and the all-night prayer vigil which helped to bring him "through." He then recalls the circumstances of his life that prompted so pagan and desperate a journey to the throne of Grace.

The overwhelming fact of Baldwin's childhood was his victimization by the white power only indirectly, as refracted through the brutality and degradation of the Harlem ghetto. The world beyond the ghetto seemed remote, and scarcely could be linked in a child's imagination to the harrowing conditions of his daily life. And yet a vague terror, transmitted through his parents to the ghetto child, attested to the power of the white world. Meanwhile, in the forefront of his consciousness was a set of fears by no means vague.

To a young boy growing up in the Harlem ghetto, damnation was a clear and present danger: "For the wages of sin were visible everywhere, in every wine-stained and urine-splashed hallway, in every clanging ambulance bell, in every scar on the faces of the pimps and their whores, in every helpless, newborn baby being brought into this danger, in every knife and pistol fight on the Avenue." To such a boy, the store-front church offered a refuge and a sanctuary from the terrors of the street. God and safety became synonymous, and the church, a part of his survival strategy.

> Robert Bone, *The Negro Novel in America* (New Haven: Yale University Press, 1958 [rev. ed. 1965]), pp. 218–19

---

**MARCUS KLEIN**        The invisibility of the Negro in America has in fact been James Baldwin's underlying metaphor ⟨. . .⟩, and when he has been most responsive to his materials he has made of invisibility, the failure of identity, a lyric of frustration and loss. What is most revealing for the case Baldwin comes to represent, however, is that the fury in his frustration and the pathos in his loss have led him, in a progress of three novels and far too many personal essays, even further from the clarity with which he began. What promised to be a dramatic recognition of the actual conditions of invisibility in his first novel, *Go Tell It on the Mountain* (1953), became a rhetoric of privileged alienation. As a Negro, Baldwin was society's victim. As a victim, he was alienated. As an alienatee, he presented himself with vast moral authority. In the space of a few years the rhetoric and the authority have done him less and less service, and he has been left to fall back on an iteration of the word "love." Love in its demonstration has become, finally, a fantasy of innocence.

The plight in invisibility has remained a plight for Baldwin, despite his uses of it as an instrument of moral authority and despite the fury in his words. His heroes are victims, caught between despair and spite, their spitefulness directed sometimes against the very sympathy which as victims they earn. They are heroes who cannot make themselves felt in the world, heroes for whom society almost provides but then doesn't quite provide a clear, felt identity. The story Baldwin tells repeatedly, in his novels, his stories, his writing for the theater, and in his essays, is of the attempt of a heroic innocent to achieve what Baldwin usually calls "identity"—"identity" is by all measure his favorite word, but on occasion the word is "manhood" or "maturity"—and the thwarting, then, of this hero by his society. The hero is prevented from entering the world. He does not achieve the definition provided by a place in the world. If sometimes in a final movement he does locate himself in a peripheral place and in a special expression of the self, in the expatriate community of Paris, perhaps, or the world of jazz, more often he finds himself shunted into one or another expression of neurosis— religious mania in *Go Tell It on the Mountain* and in Baldwin's play *The Amen Corner*, homosexuality elsewhere, a nightmare violence such as that in the first movement of *Another Country* (1962). And the hero's fulfillment stands, then, ironically and bitterly, for the quantity of his pain.

Marcus Klein, "James Baldwin: A Question of Identity," *After Alienation: American Novels at Mid-Century* (Cleveland: World Publishing Co., 1962), pp. 147–48

**STEPHEN SPENDER**      Baldwin's power is in his ability to express situations—the situation of being a Negro, and of being white, and of being human. Beyond this, he is perhaps too impatient to be a good novelist, and although he is a powerful essayist, his experiences are so colored with feelings that he seems unable to relate the thoughts which arise from his feelings to parallel situations that have given rise to other men's thoughts. Thus it seems important to him in his feelings about American Negroes that he should write as though there were no other Negroes, no other oppressed peoples anywhere in the world. He states: "Negroes do not, strictly, or legally speaking, exist in any other" country but the United States where "they are taught really to despise themselves from the moment their eyes open on the world." One suspects that for Mr. Baldwin it is sacrilege to suggest that there are Negroes outside America; and from this there follows the implication that the Negro problem is *his* problem that can only be discussed on *his* terms. Hence too his contempt for most people who, in the main, agree with him, especially for poor despised American liberals.

He has, as a Negro, a right, of course, to despise liberals, but he exploits his moral advantage too much. ⟨. . .⟩

Although Mr. Baldwin considers love is the only answer to the American race problem, it is not at all evident from his book ⟨The Fire Next Time⟩ that he loves white Americans, and at times it is even doubtful whether he loves his own people. Not that I blame him for this. What I do criticize him for is postulating a quite impossible demand as the only way of dealing with a problem that has to be solved.

Stephen Spender, "James Baldwin: Voice of a Revolution," *Partisan Review* 30, No. 2 (Summer 1963): 256–58

---

**SUSAN SONTAG**      The truth is that *Blues for Mister Charlie* isn't really about what it claims to be about. It is supposed to be about racial strife. But it is really about the anguish of tabooed sexual longings, about the crisis of identity which comes from confronting these longings, and about the rage and destructiveness (often, self-destructiveness) by which one tries to surmount this crisis. The surface may be ⟨Clifford⟩ Odets, but the interior is pure Tennessee Williams. What Baldwin has done is to take the leading theme of the serious theater of the fifties—sexual anguish— and work it up as a political play. Buried in *Blues for Mister Charlie* is the plot of several successes of the last decade: the gruesome murder of a hand- some virile young man by those who envy him his virility.

Susan Sontag, "Going to Theater, etc." (1964), *Against Interpretation and Other Essays* (New York: Farrar, Straus & Giroux, 1966), p. 155

---

**FERN MARJA ECKMAN**      James Arthur Baldwin was born in Har- lem which is geographically part of the United States but sociologically an island surrounded by the rest of the country. He was born a Negro. And to some extent this accidental conjunction of time and place has dictated his course. But it does not define who he is.

This slight, dark man is salt rubbed in the wounds of the nation's con- science. He is the shriek of the lynched. He is an accusing finger thrust in the face of white America. He is a fierce, brilliant light illuminating the unspeakable and the shameful. Gadfly and bogey man, triumphant and despairing, he has been an impassioned spokesman for the ranks of unheard Negroes, a spokesman initially appointed—and anointed—by the whites.

But first and foremost he is a writer, an American phenomenon, one of the nation's great creative artists. Like every creative artist, Baldwin mirrors the mountains, valleys and plains of his environment. In his frail person, he embodies the paradoxes and the potentials of the integration battle in the United States.

In his oratory, and sometimes, in his prose, there are apt to be passages clouded by confusion; and his political innocence has made a number of his allies apprehensive. But his emotional impact is uncompromising: harsh, violent and beautiful.

Three times now his books have secured a niche on the bestseller list, confirming his commercial attractions and enhancing his literary prestige. His old-young features with their medieval cast have been exposed frequently enough in photographs, interviews and lectures to have seemed ubiquitous. Luminaries on several continents clamor to meet him.

But all of this is part of the glittering panoply of the public Baldwin. And: "The James Baldwin the public knows is not the Jimmy I know," says his sister and secretary, Mrs. Gloria Davis Karefa-Smart.

Jimmy Baldwin, jagged as a sliver, belongs to a generation of angry, middle-aged men. He is a nonconformist, a partially reconstructed expatriate, a flagrant individualist disavowed by the bulk of middle-class Negroes, who recoil from his unorthodox conduct and even less orthodox standards.

> Fern Marja Eckman, *The Furious Passage of James Baldwin* (New York: M. Evans & Co., 1966), pp. 11–12

---

**DAVID LITTLEJOHN**     *Another Country* has, in its frantic new writer's world called New York, much of the same necessity, the same quality of desperate exorcism as Baldwin's earlier works. But things here are less under control. Almost all of the thinking, the non-imaginative thinking of Baldwin's essays is sandwiched into the fiction, bearing a suggestion that the man is now writing more from his ideas than his imagination. The piercing one-note tone of repetitiousness of so much of this long book supports this dissatisfying notion. Another dangerous sign is the confusion of narrative authority, very like the confusions of self-identity which mar so many of Baldwin's latest and weakest essays. His own opinions mingle with those of his characters, subjectivity jars with objectivity in such a way as to indicate that the author is unaware of the difference: i.e., that James Baldwin, through the 1950's the sole master of *control* in American prose, in the 1960's has begun to lose control.

What is there to salvage and prize? A number of things. More often than not, between the explosions, *Another Country* reminds the reader that James Baldwin is still one of the genuine stylists of the English language. ⟨. . .⟩

There are moments, too—especially towards the end of the novel—when Baldwin shows himself a worthy heir of Proust, suavely analyzing the mixed motives of lovers in pairs and threes and fours, their whirlpools of self-torment over the feelings of others. Eric, in particular, is so poignantly honest it wounds. And the conclusions of the book, Ida's conclusion, Eric's conclusion, are not only genuine but, for once, sympathetic and humane.

Still, all these make up—what? five percent? ten percent? of the book. Most of what we have to fall back on, finally, is the same bed of nails we began with, that four-hundred-page torture in a new-New York accent. And what good, even to a white man, is a bed of nails?

As of all "painful" works, no one reader can speculate how useful the pain may be for another. One may ask whether it is "realistic"—where there *are* such people? Baldwin, in this novel, has convinced me there are, and that they are not always the freakishly odd exceptions. The book strikes me, moreover, as precisely and exactly of its time and of its place, as much so as other honest, unfictionlike American novels such as *Herzog* or Clancy Sigal's *Going Away*. What its real value for Americans will prove, I think, for Americans who can separate the good from the bad—like so many Negro works, it is a remarkably "American" book—is that of the first open and direct statement, however unpleasant, of some underlying psychological truths of the race war, and of much else that is wrong with America as well. It reads like a record of the climactic sessions in a long, national psychoanalysis—*here* is what is really wrong, it seems to cry, for all of its own confusion, a many-men's sickness that only *one* man has been able to define, out loud.

        David Littlejohn, *Black on White: A Critical Survey of Writing by American Negroes* (New York: Grossman Publishers, 1966), pp. 130, 132–33

---

**IRVING HOWE**        Now, after having read Baldwin's new novel *Tell Me How Long the Train's Been Gone*, I have come to feel that the whole problem of Negro writing in America is far more complex that I had ever recognized, probably more complex that even Ellison had supposed, and perhaps so complex as to be, at this moment, almost beyond discussion. *Tell Me How Long the Train's Been Gone* is a remarkably bad novel, signaling the collapse of a writer of some distinction. But apart from its intrinsic qualities, it helps make clear that neither militancy nor its refusal, neither a program of aesthetic autonomy nor its denial, seems enough for the Negro novelist who wishes to transmute the life of his people into a serious piece of fiction. No program, no rhetoric, no political position makes that much difference. What does make the difference I would now be hard pressed to say, but as I have been thinking about the Negro writers I know or have read, I have come to believe that their problems are a good deal more personal than we have usually supposed. For the Negro writer, if he is indeed to be a *writer*, public posture matters less than personal identity. His problem is to reach into his true feelings, be they militant or passive, as distinct from the feelings he thinks he should have, or finds it fashionable to have, about the life of his fellow blacks. The Negro writer shares in the sufferings of an exploited race, and it would be outrageous to suppose that simply by decision he can avoid declaring his outrage; but he is also a solitary man, solitary insofar as he is a writer, solitary even more because he is a black writer, and solitary most of all if he is a black man who writes. Frequently he is detached from and in opposition to other blacks; unavoidably he must find himself troubled by his relationship to the whole looming tradition of Western literature, which is both his and never entirely his; and sooner or later he must profoundly wish to get away from racial polemic and dialectic, simply in order to reach, in his own lifetime, some completeness of being. As it seems to me, James Baldwin has come to a point where all of these problems crush down upon him and he does not quite know who he is, as writer, celebrity, or black man; so that he now suffers from the most disastrous of psychic conditions—a separation between his feelings and his voice.

Irving Howe, "James Baldwin: At Ease in Apocalypse," *Harper's Magazine* 237, No. 3 (September 1968): 95

---

**ALFRED KAZIN**     As a writer Baldwin is as obsessed by sex and family as Strindberg was, but instead of using situations for their dramatic value, Baldwin likes to pile up all possible emotional conflicts as assertions.

But for the same reason that in *Giovanni's Room* Baldwin made everybody white just to show that he could, and in *Tell Me How Long the Train's Been Gone* transferred the son-father quarrel to a quarrel with a brother, so one feels about *Another Country* that Baldwin writes fiction in order to use up his private difficulties; even his fiction piles up the atmosphere of raw emotion that is his literary standby. ⟨. . .⟩

But in *Notes of a Native Son, Nobody Knows My Name, The Fire Next Time*, Baldwin dropped the complicated code for love difficulties he uses in his novels and simplified himself into an "angry Black" very powerfully indeed—and this just before Black nationalists were to turn on writers like him. The character who calls himself "James Baldwin" in *his* nonfiction novel is more professionally enraged, more doubtfully an evangelist for his people, than the actual James Baldwin, a very literary mind indeed. But there is in *Notes of a Native Son* a genius for bringing many symbols together, an instinctive association with the 1943 Harlem riot, the streets of smashed plate glass, that stems from the all too understandable fascination of the Negro with the public sources of his fate. The emphasis is on heat, fire, anger, the sense of being hemmed in and suffocated; the words are tensed into images that lacerate and burn. Reading Baldwin's essays, we are suddenly past the discordancy that has plagued his fiction—a literal problem of conflict, for Baldwin's fiction shows him trying to transpose facts into fiction without sacrificing the emotional capital that has been his life.

Alfred Kazin, *Bright Book of Life: American Novelists and Storytellers from Hemingway to Mailer* (Boston: Little, Brown, 1973), pp. 222–24

---

**JOYCE CAROL OATES**     A spare, slender narrative, told first-person by a 19-year-old black girl named Tish, *If Beale Street Could Talk* manages to be many things at the same time. It is economically, almost poetically constructed, and may certainly be read as a kind of allegory, which refuses conventional outbursts of violence, preferring to stress the provisional, tentative nature of our lives. ⟨. . .⟩

Baldwin certainly risked a great deal by putting his complex narrative, which involves a number of important characters, into the mouth of a young girl. Yet Tish's voice comes to seem absolutely natural and we learn to know her from the inside out. Even her flights of poetic fancy—involving rather subtle speculations upon the nature of male-female relationships, or black-white relationships, as well as her articulation of what it feels like to be pregnant—are convincing. Also convincing is Baldwin's insistence upon the primacy of emotions like love, hate, or terror: it is not sentimentality, but basic psychology, to acknowledge the fact that one person will die, and another survive simply because one has not the guarantee of a fundamental human bond, like love, while the other has. ⟨. . .⟩

*If Beale Street Could Talk* is a moving, painful story. It is so vividly human and so obviously based upon reality, that it strikes us as timeless—an art that has not the slightest need of esthetic tricks, and even less need of fashionable apocalytic excesses.

Joyce Carol Oates, [Review of *If Beale Street Could Talk*], *New York Times Book Review*, 19 May 1974, pp. 1–2

**SHIRLEY S. ALLEN**     From the very beginning of the novel ⟨*Go Tell It on the Mountain*⟩ Baldwin clearly indicates the central importance of religious symbolism. The title, taken from a Negro spiritual, suggests not only the basic Christian setting of the action, but also the kind of symbolism we are to expect. In different versions of the folk hymn the command, "Go tell it," refers to the good news (gospel) that "Jesus Christ is born" or to the message of Moses to the Pharaoh, "Let my people go." The ambiguity of the allusion in the title is intentional and also suggests the unity of Old Testament and New Testament faith that is characteristic of the Christian belief described in the novel—the teachings of a sect formed from Baptist practices and Calvinist doctrines, grounded in frequent reading of the King James translation of the Bible, and influenced by the needs, hopes, and artistic expression of Negro slaves. ⟨. . .⟩ Baldwin's use of Biblical allusion in the title and the first epigraph to give symbolic meaning to John's conversion and to interpret the event is typical of his use of symbolism throughout the novel. Each of the three parts has a title and two epigraphs referring to the Bible or Christian hymns, and each of the prayers in Part Two begins with a quotation from a hymn. Two of Gabriel's sermons, based on Biblical texts, are paraphrased at some length. The thoughts and spoken words of almost all the characters are larded with passages from the King James version, and the major characters are identified with their favorite texts of scripture. The doctrines, ritual, songs, and visual symbols of the Baptist church are equally pervasive in the words and events of the novel.

But all this religious apparatus, like the central scene of the tarry service itself, is used not simply as psychological and social milieu for the action, but also to give symbolic expression and archetypal meaning to the characters and events. Biblical allusion in Go Tell It on the Mountain serves some of the same purposes as the Homeric myth in Ulysses and the Olympic paraphernalia in The Centaur, but Baldwin's use of the religious apparatus is more like that of Dostoyevsky in the Brothers Karamazov than that of Joyce and Updike in one important respect: the symbolism arises naturally out of the setting. This very integration of symbolic apparatus and milieu is perhaps the reason critics have missed the symbolism—a case of not seeing the forest in the trees. ⟨. . .⟩

The effect of this religious symbolism is to keep the reader aware of the universal elements in John's struggle so that its significance will not be lost amid the specific details and particular persons complicating his conflict. The symbolism prevents us, for example, from mistaking John's peculiar problem as a black taking his place in a society dominated by whites for the more basic problem, common to all humanity, of a child taking his place in adult society. The symbolism also keeps us from being sidetracked by the specific personality of Gabriel or the fact that he is not John's real father, since he is named for the angel of the Annunciation and therefore symbolically is the agency of fatherhood. We are to see John in the larger view as a human child struggling against dependency and finding a sense of his own selfhood through the initiation rite practiced in his community, even though Baldwin has fully realized that struggle in the specific circum-stances of Harlem, the fully rounded human characteristics of the Grimes family, and the particular heritage of American Negro religion.

> Shirley S. Allen, "Religious Symbolism and Psychic Reality in Baldwin's Go Tell It on the Mountain," CLA Journal 19, No. 2 (December 1975): 175, 177–79

---

**TRUDIER HARRIS**      Sex that was transformed into godhead in If Beale Street Could Talk is eliminated altogether in Just Above My Head. Realizing that he perhaps could not keep his characters at the level of the gods and still enable them to live in this world, Baldwin initially returned to the worldliness of sex in Just Above My Head as well as to some of the familiar conflicts between males and females that were visible in his earlier fiction. In the conclusion of the novel, however, Baldwin leaves Julia, though in this world, yet beyond the petty realities of role playing and sex. The brotherhood he had underscored with Tish, Fonny, their families, and the Puerto Ricans in *If Beale Street Could Talk* is picked up again with the extended families in *Just Above My Head*, particularly as it is manifested at the end of the novel with Hall's family and with Julia and Jimmy.

Having moved beyond sex, wives, mothers, sisters, and lovers, the major black male and female characters in *Just Above My Head* are truly at peace when they have transcended physical contact (though Hall has not yet transcended desire) and can also exist at an implied larger-than-life level. Julia has gone through many storms to arrive at the calm she manifests on the day of the barbecue. And Hall has gone through a lot to realize that Julia can no longer be possessed physically. They have given up each other's bodies for mutual respect and peaceful coexistence. Lest we conclude that such a platonic view might suggest the end of the family, keep in mind that Hall still has Ruth and his children, Odessa and Tony. He has them, and he has Julia. Somewhere in the midst of that seeming overdose is the suggestion that perhaps the extended family, the communal family, minimizes the acute tension that individuals feel who are isolated in nuclear families. Remember, again, that Florence and Elizabeth are in many ways isolated; especially is this true of Florence and her desire to escape from "niggers." Ruth voluntarily gave up her repressive nuclear family, and Ida voluntarily left Harlem to escape what she imagined would be confinement from her environment if she remained within her nuclear family. The concept of the extended family—across oceans, across nations and nationalities, across sexes—as a viable alternative to the restrictions of the nuclear family surfaced in *If Beale Street Could Talk* with Fonny and Frank becoming a part of the Rivers family, and with the Puerto Ricans in New York adopting Tish and Fonny. Conflicts that may arise ultimately seem small because the support group is larger; such is the case with the extended families in *Just Above My Head*. Before the establishment of peace, however, it must be clear who can touch whom, who must play which roles for whom, and what all expectations are. It is only after all those things have been clarified that Hall and Julia can be so peaceful with each other. They have sacrificed parochial experience for international experience, and they have thereby broken free of some of the restraints that so characterized the interactions between black men and black women in Baldwin's earlier fiction. Their situation does not allow us to conclude that the black man has completely given up his desire for mastery over black women; it does suggest, however, that at least one kind of black woman has escaped from the limitations of that desire. Hall and Julia may or may not point the way to the future in Baldwin's works, but they do show that at least one healthy pattern of resolution to the conflicts between black men and black women in Baldwin's fiction has been meticulously worked out.

> Trudier Harris, *Black Women in the Fiction of James Baldwin* (Knoxville: University of Tennessee Press, 1985), pp. 210–11

---

**JANE CAMPBELL**      Baldwin transmutes the messianic myth into that of an artist-priest whose visionary powers allow transcendence of oppression so that she or he can ultimately change history. To Baldwin, the personal and racial past are inseparable; therefore, to grasp racial history, one must first confront personal history. Beyond knowledge lies change, and within each sensitive intellectual lodge the tools for transforming history. *Go Tell It on the Mountain*, like *Invisible Man*, exemplifies distrust of collective effort in favor of individual action. Moreover, although Baldwin's work anticipates the urge to explore and reconstruct history, an urge permeating Afro-American literature of the sixties, seventies, and eighties, *Go Tell It on the Mountain* does not reckon with African history or culture.

The introspection Baldwin demands of his leaders prohibits him from employing the romance, with its de-emphasis on subjectivity. Instead, he turns to the confessional mode to convey his protagonist's guilt, confession, and transcendence. By using flashbacks disguised as prayers to present personal histories, Baldwin underscores the spiritual dimensions of those histories, at the same time focusing on the points of congruence between the personal and racial past. Finally, one must applaud Baldwin's recognition of the centrality of religion in black life and his ingenuity in employing a fictional mode that clearly suggests spiritual and religious concerns.

In a sense, Baldwin's entire canon might be called confessional, but critics have done surprisingly little to illuminate Baldwin's use of the form. Most refer to *Go Tell It on the Mountain* as an autobiographical novel, based on the author's now legendary conversion to the ministry. But to term a novel "autobiographical" tells only part of the story; to some extent, most fiction may derive from the writer's life. The term autobiographical, though it does link episodes and characters to their creator, fails to elucidate much about the way the artist transforms these elements into art. Moreover, authors often augment or alter the actual when they transmute it into fiction. Baldwin, for example, as quoted by Fern M. Eckman, says that Richard, John Grimes' biological father, is "completely imaginary," but at least one critic has theorized that Richard's characterization is unsuccessful because Baldwin was too close to his material to achieve aesthetic distance. Looking at *Go Tell It on the Mountain* as confessional probably discloses more about Baldwin's transformation of life into art than viewing the work as autobiography.

> Jane Campbell, "Retreat into the Self: Ralph Ellison's *Invisible Man* and James Baldwin's *Go Tell It on the Mountain*," *Mythic Black Fiction: The Transformation of History* (Knoxville: University of Tennessee Press, 1986), pp. 101–2

---

**HORACE A. PORTER**      There is, of course, genuine merit, even if shrouded in the thick smoke of his fiery black rhetoric, in certain of his insights about America's vision of itself. There are, for example, as he observes on several occasions, people in the world who exist far beyond the confines of the American imagination. But what I call the tragedy concerns Baldwin's abdication of his responsibility as a serious writer—a serious writer like Henry James—in the course of his decision, enthusiasm, and willingness to assume the role of racial spokesman and representative. An accomplished writer and cosmopolite, Baldwin knows with acute awareness how hopelessly interdependent the world has become. If America is the premier example of "retarded adolescence," as Baldwin calls it, what country, if not his own, would he suggest even figuratively has achieved adulthood or maturity— his beloved France, England, Brazil, Nigeria? Furthermore, in "Everybody's Protest Novel" Baldwin argues passionately that a human being is considerably more than "merely a member of a Society or a Group or a deplorable conundrum to be explained by science." But he willingly becomes a representative of people of color around the globe: "What they don't know about me is what they don't know about Nicaragua." ⟨. . .⟩

It almost seems as though the gods conspire against Baldwin. On the one hand, they grant him the rare and priceless gift of supreme literary intelligence. On the other, they provide a set of personal circumstances, including the historical moment, that leads him to assume the arduous task of illuminating and seeking to solve the so-called American dilemma. They made him black. To paraphrase Louis Armstrong singing "What Did I Do to Be So Black and Blue," "His only sin was in his skin." Given Baldwin's Harlem boyhood of poverty and anonymity, it makes perfect sense and it is certainly to his eternal credit that he strongly identifies with black Americans, and that he, so to speak, cut his teeth on *Uncle Tom's Cabin* and *Native Son*. It is understandable that he was inclined to exhort and persuade the hard-hearted and to articulate the rage of the disesteemed. The temper of the times, the civil rights movement, gave him the historical stage on which to voice with moral clarity and authority what the consequences of America's moral evasion and racial bigotry would be.

But, finally, the threatening possibility that he clairvoyantly sees in "Everybody's Protest Novel" ensnarls him too. With the publication of *The Fire Next Time*, Baldwin is typecast as an angry spokesman—"a black Tom Paine," as *Time* magazine put it. The limitation that he had diagnosed in "Everybody's Protest Novel"—a limitation imposing itself on the writer from without and simultaneously corroborating or inscribing itself from deep within—imposed itself on him.

> Horace A. Porter, *Stealing the Fire: The Art and Protest of James Baldwin* (Middletown, CT: Wesleyan University Press, 1989), pp. 164–65

---

**MEL WATKINS**      As a writer, then, Baldwin is part of the tradition of black-American polemical essayists that include David Walker, Henry Highland Garnet, Frederick Douglass, Booker T. Washington, and W. E. B. Du Bois. But he is just as much a part of the tradition of American Romantic moralists—a group that includes Ralph Waldo Emerson, Henry David Thoreau, and John Jay Chapman. This dual approach, the ability to assume the voice of black as well as white Americans, accounts, in great part, for his popularity and acceptance among Americans on both sides of the racial issue.

His appeal to America's mainstream society notwithstanding, he became, as Albert Murray pointed out in *The Omni-Americans* (1970), a hero of "the Negro revolution, a citizen spokesman, as eloquent . . . as was citizen polemicist Tom Paine in the Revolution of '76." But, most often, he did not, as Murray asserts, "write about the economic and social conditions of Harlem." Quite the contrary, Eldridge Cleaver was more accurate when ⟨. . .⟩ he wrote that Baldwin's work "is void of a political, economic, or even a social reference." For Baldwin's technique was to write through events, to penetrate the external veneer of sociological generality and probe the darker underside—"the real world" that Jesse Jackson alluded to at the 1988 Democratic convention—focusing finally on the enigmas that resided beneath the social and economic, enigmas that ultimately plagued his own psyche as well as our own. His influence and popularity, then, depended largely on the extent to which his psyche corresponded to the mass American psyche.

Mel Watkins, "An Appreciation," *James Baldwin: The Legacy*, ed. Quincy Troupe (New York: Simon & Schuster, 1989), p. 117

# ▨ *Bibliography*

*Go Tell It on the Mountain*. 1953.

*Notes of a Native Son*. 1955.

*Giovanni's Room*. 1956.

*Nobody Knows My Name: More Notes of a Native Son*. 1961.

*Another Country*. 1962.

*The Fire Next Time*. 1963.

*Nothing Personal* (with Richard Avedon). 1964.

*Blues for Mr. Charlie*. 1964.

*Going to Meet the Man*. 1965.

*The Amen Corner*. 1968.

*Tell Me How Long the Train's Been Gone*. 1968.

*An Open Letter to My Sister, Miss Angela Davis*. 1970.

*A Rap on Race* (with Margaret Mead). 1971.

*No Name in the Street*. 1972.

*One Day, When I Was Lost: A Scenario Based on Alex Haley's* The Autobiography of Malcolm X. 1972.

*A Dialogue* (with Nikki Giovanni). 1973.

*If Beale Street Could Talk*. 1974.

*Little Man, Little Man: A Story of Childhood*. 1976.

*The Devil Finds Work: An Essay*. 1976.

*Just Above My Head*. 1979.

*Jimmy's Blues: Selected Poems*. 1983.

*The Price of the Ticket: Collected Nonfiction 1948–1985*. 1985.

*The Evidence of Things Not Seen*. 1985.

*Gypsy and Other Poems.* 1989.

*Conversations with James Baldwin.* Ed. Fred L. Standley and Louis H. Pratt.
     1989.

# Ralph Ellison
## *1914–1994*

RALPH WALDO ELLISON was born on March 1, 1914, in Oklahoma City, Oklahoma. His father, Lewis Ellison, was a construction worker and trades-man who died when Ellison was three. His mother, Ida Millsap, worked as a domestic servant but was active in radical politics for many years. Ellison thrived on the discarded magazines and phonograph records she brought home from the white households where she worked. He attended Douglass High School in Oklahoma City, where he learned the soprano saxophone, trumpet, and other instruments, playing both jazz and light classical music.

In 1933 Ellison began studying music at the Tuskegee Institute in Ala-bama. He remained there for three years before coming to New York in 1936, where he held a number of odd jobs while continuing to study music and sculpture. In New York he met Langston Hughes and Richard Wright, who gave him great encouragement in his writing. Ellison's short stories, essays, and reviews began appearing in the *Antioch Review*, the *New Masses*, and many other magazines and journals in the late 1930s. At this time his interest in social justice attracted him to the Communist party, although he would later repudiate it. Ellison gained a modicum of financial security in 1938 when he was hired by the Federal Writers' Project to gather folklore and present it in literary form. The four years he spent at this work enriched his own writing by providing source material that would be incorporated into his own fiction.

In 1943, wishing to help in the war effort, Ellison joined the merchant marine. The next year he received a Rosenwald Foundation Fellowship to write a novel; although he mapped out a plot, he failed to finish the work (one section was published as a short story, "Flying Home"). After the war he went to a friend's farm in Vermont to recuperate, and it was here that he conceived the novel that would establish him as a major writer—*Invisible Man*. He worked on the book for five years, and it was finally published in 1952. This long novel is both a historical biography of the black man in America and an allegory of man's quest for identity. *Invisible Man* received the National Book Award for fiction in 1953 and is now regarded as one of the most distinguished American novels of the century. *Shadow and Act* (1964), Ellison's second book, is a collection of personal essays about literature, folklore, jazz, and the author's life.

Even before finishing *Invisible Man*, Ellison had conceived the idea for another novel. Although he published several segments of it as short stories and read others on television and at lectures, the work remained unfinished at the time of his death; a large portion of it was destroyed by a fire at Ellison's summer home in Massachusetts in 1967. Because he did not advocate black separatism, Ellison fell out of sympathy with the black writers and thinkers of the 1960s; but over the last two decades he has again become a much sought-after lecturer on college campuses. A second collection of essays, *Going to the Territory,* was published in 1986.

Ralph Ellison held visiting professorships at Yale, Bard College, the University of Chicago, and elsewhere. From 1970 to 1979 he was Albert Schweitzer Professor in the Humanities at New York University, later becoming an emeritus professor there. He held a fellowship of the American Academy of Arts and Letters in Rome from 1955 to 1957, and received the United States Medal of Freedom in 1969. He was a charter member of the National Council of the Arts, has served as trustee of the John F. Kennedy Center for the Performing Arts, and was honorary consultant in American Letters at the Library of Congress. Ellison was married twice, but details of his first marriage are unavailable; in 1946 he married Fanny McConnell. Ralph Ellison died in New York City on April 16, 1994.

# ◈ *Critical Extracts*

**SAUL BELLOW**        I was keenly aware, as I read this book ⟨*Invisible Man*⟩, of a very significant kind of independence in the writing. For there is a "way" for Negro novelists to go at their problems, just as there are Jewish or Italian "ways." Mr. Ellison has not adopted a minority tone. If he had done so, he would have failed to establish a true middle-of-consciousness for everyone.

Negro Harlem is at once primitive and sophisticated; it exhibits the extremes of instinct and civilization as few other American communities do. If a writer dwells on the peculiarity of this, he ends with an exotic effect. And Mr. Ellison is not exotic. For him this balance of instinct and culture or civilization is not a Harlem matter; it is *the* matter, German, French, Russian, American, universal, a matter very little understood. It is thought that Negroes and other minority people, kept under in the great status battle, are in the instinct cellar of dark enjoyment. This imagined enjoyment provokes envious rage and murder; and then it is a large portion of human nature itself which becomes the fugitive murderously pursued. In our society Man—Himself—is idolized and publicly worshipped, but the single individual must hide himself underground and try to save his desires, his thoughts, his soul, in invisibility. He must return to himself, learning self-acceptance and rejecting all that threatens to deprive him of his manhood.

This is what I make of *Invisible Man*. It is not by any means faultless; I don't think the hero's experiences in the Communist party are as original in conception as other parts of the book, and his love affair with a white woman is all too brief, but it is an immensely moving novel and it has greatness.

Saul Bellow, "Man Underground," *Commentary* 13, No. 6 (June 1952): 609

---

**EARL H. ROVIT**    The most obvious comment one can make about Ralph Ellison's *Invisible Man* is that it is a profoundly comic work. But the obvious is not necessarily either simple or self-explanatory, and it seems to me that the comic implications of Ellison's novel are elusive and provocative enough to warrant careful examination both in relation to the total effect of the novel itself and the American cultural pattern from which it derives. ⟨. . .⟩

First it should be noted that Ellison's commitment to what Henry James has termed "the American joke" has been thoroughly deliberate and undisguised. Ellison once described penetratingly the ambiguous *locus* of conflicting forces within which the American artist has had always to work: "For the ex-colonials, the declaration of an American identity meant the assumption of a mask, and it imposed not only the discipline of national self-consciousness, it gave Americans an ironic awareness of the joke that always lies between appearance and reality, between the discontinuity of social tradition and that sense of the past which clings to the mind. And perhaps even an awareness of the joke that society is man's creation, not God's."

This kind of ironic awareness may contain bitterness and may even become susceptible to the heavy shadow of despair, but the art which it produces has been ultimately comic. It will inevitably probe the masks of identity and value searching relentlessly for some deeper buried reality, but it will do this while accepting the fundamental necessity for masks and the impossibility of ever discovering an essential face beneath a mask. That is to say, this comic stance will accept with the same triumphant gesture both the basic absurdity of all attempts to impose meaning on the chaos of life, and the necessary converse of this, the ultimate significance of absurdity itself.

Ellison's *Invisible Man* is comic in this sense almost in spite of its overtly satirical interests and its excursions into the broadly farcical. Humorous as many of its episodes are in themselves—the surreal hysteria of the scene at the Golden Day, the hero's employment at the Liberty Paint Company, or the expert dissection of political entanglements in Harlem—these are the materials which clothe Ellison's joke and which, in turn, suggest the shape by which the joke can be comprehended. The pith of Ellison's comedy reverberates on a level much deeper than these incidents, and as in all true humor, the joke affirms and denies simultaneously—accepts and rejects with the same uncompromising passion, leaving not a self-cancelling neutralization of momentum, but a sphere of moral conquest, a humanized cone of light at the very heart of the heart of darkness. *Invisible Man,* as Ellison has needlessly insisted in rebuttal to those critics who would treat the novel as fictionalized sociology or as a dramatization of archetypal images, is an artist's attempt to create a *form.* And fortunately Ellison has been quite explicit in describing what he means by *form;* in specific reference to the improvisation of the jazz-musician he suggests that form represents "a definition of his identity: as an individual, as a member of the collectivity, and as a link in the chain of tradition." But note that each of these definitions of identity must be individually exclusive and mutually contradictory on any logical terms. Because of its very pursuit after the uniqueness of individuality, the successful definition of an individual must define out the possibilities of generalization into "collectivity" or "tradition." But herein for Ellison in his embrace of a notion of fluid amorphous identity lies the real morality and humor in mankind's art and men's lives—neither of which have much respect for the laws of formal logic.

Earl H. Rovit, "Ralph Ellison and the American Comic Tradition," *Wisconsin Studies in Contemporary Literature* 1, No. 3 (Fall 1960): 34–35

**JONATHAN BAUMBACH**     I hesitate to call Ralph Ellison's *Invisible Man* (1952) a Negro novel, though of course it is written by a Negro and is centrally concerned with the experiences of a Negro. The appellation is not so much inaccurate as it is misleading. A novelist treating the invisibility and phantasmagoria of the Negro's life in this "democracy" is, if he tells the truth, necessarily writing a very special kind of book. Yet if his novel is interesting only because of its specialness, he has not violated the surface of his subject; he has not, after all, been serious. Despite the differences in their external concerns, Ellison has more in common as a novelist with Joyce, Melville, Camus, Kafka, West, and Faulkner than he does with other serious writers like James Baldwin and Richard Wright. To concentrate on the idiom of a serious novel, no matter how distinctive its peculiarities, is to depreciate it, to minimize the universality of its implications. Though the protagonist of *Invisible Man* is a southern Negro, he is, in Ellison's rendering, profoundly all of us.

Despite its obvious social implications, Ellison's novel is a modern gothic, a Candide-like picaresque set in a dimly familiar nightmare landscape called the United States. Like *The Catcher in the Rye*, *A Member of the Wedding*, and *The Adventures of Augie March*, Ellison's novel chronicles a series of initiatory experiences through which its naïve hero learns, to his disillusion and horror, the way of the world. However, unlike these other novels of passage, *Invisible Man* takes place, for the most part, in the uncharted spaces between the conscious and the unconscious, in the semilit darkness where nightmare verges on reality and the external world has all the aspects of a disturbing dream. Refracted by satire, at times, cartooned, Ellison's world is at once surreal and real, comic and tragic, grotesque and normal—our world viewed in its essentials rather than its externals.

The Negro's life in our white land and time is, as Ellison knows it, a relentless unreality, unreal in that the Negro as a group is loved, hated, persecuted, feared, and envied, while as an individual he is unfelt, unheard, unseen—to all intents and purposes invisible. The narrator, who is also the novel's central participant, never identifies himself by name. Though he experiences several changes of identity in the course of the novel, Ellison's hero exists to the reader as a man without an identity, an invisible "I." In taking on a succession of identities, the invisible hero undergoes an increasingly intense succession of disillusioning experiences, each one paralleling and anticipating the one following it. The hero's final loss of illusion forces him underground into the coffin (and womb) of the earth to be either finally buried or finally reborn.

Jonathan Baumbach, "Nightmare of a Native Son," *The Landscape of Nightmare: Studies in the Contemporary American Novel* (New York: New York University Press, 1965), pp. 68–69

**EDWARD MARGOLIES**      Not surprisingly, Ellison's understanding of his early life corresponds to his definition of Negro jazz. And ultimately it is jazz, and blues especially, that becomes the aesthetic mainspring of his writing. If literature serves as a ritualistic means of ordering experience, so does music, as Ellison well understands. And it is more to the rites of the jazz band than to the teachings of Kenneth Burke or the influences of Hemingway, Stein, Eliot, Malraux, or Conrad (persons whom Ellison mentions as literary ancestors and preceptors) that Ellison owes the structure and informing ideas of his novel. Particularly relevant is the attention Ellison casts on the jazz soloist. Within and against a frame of chordal progressions and rhythmic patterns, the soloist is free to explore a variety of ideas and emotions. But this freedom is not absolute. The chordal background of the other musicians demands a discipline that the soloist dare not breach. He is as much a part of the whole as he is an individual, and he may well lose himself in the whole before he recovers his individual identity. Finally, music, however tragic its message, is an affirmation of life, a celebration of the indomitable human spirit, in that it imposes order and form on the chaos of experience. ⟨. . .⟩

Since the blues, according to Ellison, is by its very nature a record of past wrongs, pains, and defeats, it serves to define the singer as one who has suffered, and in so doing it has provided him with a history. As the novel ⟨*Invisible Man*⟩ develops, the hero takes on the role of a Negro Everyman, whose adventures and cries of woe and laughter become the history of a people. As a high-school boy in the South, he is a "Tom"— little better than a darky entertainer; in college, a Booker T. Washington accommodationist. When he moves North, he works as a nonunion laborer and then flirts for a while with Communism. Finally, he becomes a Rinehart, Ellison's word for the unattached, alienated, urban Negro who deliberately endeavors to manipulate the fantasies of whites and Negroes to his own advantage. But besides being a kind of symbolic recapitulation of Negro

history, the blues structure of the novel suggests a philosophy of history as
well—something outside racial determinism, progress, or various ideologies,
something indefinably human, unexpected and perhaps nonrational.

> Edward Margolies, "History as Blues: Ralph Ellison's *Invisible Man*," *Native Sons:
> A Critical Study of Twentieth-Century Negro American Authors* (Philadelphia: J. B.
> Lippincott Co., 1968), pp. 130, 133

---

**BARBARA CHRISTIAN**    Unlike Wright and other notable black
writers, Ellison is the spokesman for the "infinite possibilities" that he feels
are inherent in the condition of being an artist rather than a Negro artist.
He repeatedly states in his essays that his primary concern is not the social
but rather the aesthetic responsibilities of the writer. ⟨. . .⟩

There is one word that crops up repeatedly in both the essays and *Invisible
Man* and which is at the base of Ellison's aesthetic beliefs. That word is
*myth*, the magical transformer of life. Influenced by T. S. Eliot whom he
calls his literary ancestor, Ellison combines the literary past and the memory
and culture of the individual with the present, thus placing the contemporary
writer alongside the other men who have written in the English language.
Baldwin stresses the fact that the writer creates out of his own experience.
Ellison would add that one writes out of one's experience as understood
through one's knowledge of self, culture, and literature. Self, in Ellison's
case, refers to his own past and background, culture to the American culture
and more specifically to Negro American culture, and literature to the
entire range of works in European literature that help to make up Western
sensibility.

Even Ellison's name itself is steeped in myth as he points out in the
essay, "Hidden Names and Complex Fate." His father had named him after
Ralph Waldo Emerson and Ellison recalls that "much later after I began to
write and work with words, I came to suspect that my father had been aware
of the suggestive powers of names and the magic involved in naming." The
name *Ralph Waldo* indeed had magic for it enabled Ellison to see the power
of the myth and to envision the role that myth could play in achieving his
aim which was, as he put it, "to add to literature the wonderful American
speech and idiom and to bring into range as fully as possible the complex
reality of American experience as it shaped and was shaped by the lives of
my own people." Myths in order to be preserved and appreciated must be

written down and Ellison, in his comments on Hemingway and Faulkner, is constantly aware that one element of the American past is sorely missing from most American literature. As Ralph Waldo Emerson could merge the myths and attitudes of New England into his philosophy of Transcendentalism, Ralph Waldo Ellison would merge that essential element, the nature of black folklore and life style, into American literature—and myth could be the carrier.

Barbara Christian, "Ralph Ellison: A Critical Study," *Black Expression: Essays by and about Black Americans in the Creative Arts*, ed. Addison Gayle, Jr. (New York: Weybright & Talley, 1969), pp. 354–55

---

**TONY TANNER**      In the introduction to his essays (*Shadow and Act*), Ralph Ellison, recalling the circumstances of his youth, stresses the significance of the fact that while Oklahoman jazz musicians were developing 'a freer, more complex and driving form of jazz, my friends and I were exploring an idea of human versatility and possibility which went against the barbs or over the palings of almost every fence which those who controlled social and political power had erected to restrict our roles in the life of the country.' The fact that these musicians working with 'tradition, imagination and the sounds and emotions around them', could create something new which was both free yet recognizably formed (this is the essence of improvisation) was clearly of the first importance for Ralph Ellison; the ideas of versatility and possibility which he and his friends were exploring provide the ultimate subject-matter, and nourish the style, of his one novel to date, *Invisible Man* (1952), a novel which in many ways is seminal for subsequent American fiction. His title may owe something to H. G. Wells's novel *The Invisible Man*, for the alienated Griffin in Wells's novel also comes to realize 'what a helpless absurdity an Invisible Man was—in a cold and dirty climate and a crowded, civilized city' and there is a very suggestive scene in which he tries to assemble an identity, which is at the same time a disguise, from the wigs, masks, artificial noses, and clothes of Omniums, the large London store. It would not be surprising if Wells's potentially very probing little novel about the ambiguity involved in achieving social 'identity' had stayed in Ellison's extremely literate memory. But if it did so it would be because Ellison's experience as a Negro had taught him a profounder sort of invisibility than any chemically induced vanishing trick.

As the narrator says in the opening paragraph, it is as though he lives surrounded by mirrors of distorting glass, so that other people do not see him but only his surroundings, or reflections of themselves, or their fantasies. It is an aspect of recent American fiction that work coming from members of so-called minority groups has proved to be relevant and applicable to the situation of people not sharing their immediate racial experience or, as it may be, sexual inclination; and *Invisible Man,* so far from being limited to an expression of an anguish and injustice experienced peculiarly by Negroes, is quite simply the most profound novel about American identity written since the war.

Tony Tanner, *City of Words: American Fiction 1950–1970* (New York: Harper & Row, 1971), p. 50

**ARTHUR P. DAVIS**      Among Ellison's earliest publications was a short story which came out in 1944 called "Flying Home." In this short fiction we have an introduction to the techniques Ellison was later to use superbly in his novel. A narrative concerning an incident in the Air Force school for Negro pilots in the Deep South, the work makes use of realistic details, a flashback technique, the Greek myth of Icarus, a Negro folk story, and miscellaneous symbols of the modern world. Ellison makes the whole story an extended metaphor of the Negro's place in American society.

The simple story concerns Todd, a Negro pilot trainee in Alabama who flies upward too precipitously, and strikes a buzzard (Jim Crow), and crashes on the property of a white landowner. When Todd regains consciousness, the first persons he sees are Jefferson, an old Negro sharecropper, and a boy, whom Jefferson sends for a physician. In the interim the old man needles the pilot. Why you want to fly, Boy, he asks, in effect, you *could* get shot for a buzzard. Note the emphasis on *buzzard,* a bird symbolizing the past because it eats dead things. Note also the old stay-in-your-place attitude held not only by whites but by Negroes as well. In his way Jefferson is a buzzard, resenting this fancy new-type Negro.

Jefferson then tells Todd a folk story known to most Negroes: the story of his going to Heaven where he was given six-foot angels' wings. Jefferson, however, flew too fast and dangerously and was thrown out of Heaven. The implications of the story are obvious, and the old man's taunting laughter drives Todd into a screaming rage: "Can I help it because they won't actually let us fly? Maybe we are a bunch of buzzards feeding on a dead horse, but we can hope to be eagles, can't we?"

At the end of the story the white landowner brings in orderlies from a mental institution. "You all know you cain't let the Nigguh get up that high without going crazy. The Nigguh brain ain't built right for high altitudes."

Here is a brilliant mélange of realism, folk story, and symbolism, with a touch of surrealism at the end—the kind of fusion found on a grand scale in *Invisible Man*.

> Arthur P. Davis, *From the Dark Tower: Afro-American Writers 1900 to 1960* (Washington, DC: Howard University Press, 1974), pp. 209–10

**WILLI REAL**     It is not uncommon to regard short stories as precursors of more comprehensive fictional works or even merely as by-products of a novelist's career. This view seems confirmed by some of Ralph Ellison's pieces of short fiction. His first story, "Slick Gonna Learn," is an excerpt from an unpublished novel, the famous "Battle Royal," first chapter of Ellison's *Invisible Man*, goes back to an earlier short story of that name, and his stories "Flying Home" and "King of the Bingo Game" are said to anticipate major themes of *Invisible Man* as well. Yet it is still difficult if not impossible to say whether Ellison will be remembered as a novelist or as a novelist *and* a short story writer. ⟨. . .⟩

The protagonist of "King of the Bingo Game" is neither an ideal hero nor an anti-hero. Like all other characters both black and white, he is unnamed (his wife Laura being the only exception in the story). He was reared in the South and, like so many other people during the Great Migration, he walked the traditional road to freedom: like the protagonist of *Invisible Man* and like Ellison himself, he left the rural South where black solidarity was greater but white domination also more rigid, for the more industrialized North. But instead of finding the Promised Land there, he has to experience the depersonalizing influence of Northern slums where human emotions are crippled and where folk ties are eroded. As he possesses no birth certificate which is called by Deutsch a petty, bureaucratic technicality, he is officially a non-person, a nobody unable to get a job. Thus his personal situation which is also that of the protagonist in "Slick Gonna Learn," is representative of that of so many people living in a slum. It means being caught in a vicious circle which is characterized by poverty, denial of individuality, denial of work, denial of medical care, death. ⟨. . .⟩

The aimlessness and senselessness of the protagonist's way of acting, the cyclic structure of the story is enhanced by a literary device whose full effect is only revealed by considering the context of this piece of short fiction as a whole: irony.

Willi Real, "Ralph Ellison: 'King of the Bingo Game,'" *The Black American Short Story in the 20th Century*, ed. Peter Bruck (Amsterdam: B. R. Grüner Publishing Co., 1977), pp. 111, 115, 122

**RICHARD FINHOLT**     Ellison, after Poe, is the American writer most self-consciously committed to the idea of the mind thinking, of the mind, that is, as the ultimate source of transcendence or salvation. But he is also the inheritor of a wellspring of emotional pain, the collective black experience in America, that has received its traditional artistic expression in the blues beat and lyric. ⟨. . .⟩

In fact, the novel ⟨*Invisible Man*⟩ amounts to a critique of both the intellectual and the emotional dimensions of the American experience. The Brotherhood (an obvious pseudonym for the Communist Party), which prides itself on its "reasonable point of view" and "scientific approach to society," represents the *head* of the social structure, as do also such characters as Bledsoe, Norton, Emerson, and all who think without feeling; and characters like Trueblood, Emerson Jr., Lucius Brockway, Tarp, Tod Clifton, and Ras, all those who feel without thinking, represent the *heart*. Given the two dimensions, the invisible man's problem, as for the heroes of the other writers studied here, is "How to Be!" And, as with the others, salvation is the attainment of a balance, of a unification of mind and body, thought and feeling, idea and action, that forms a pattern of existence with the potential to transcend the "biological morality" (Audrey's term) imposed from within and the social morality imposed from without.

Melville saw all men "enveloped in whale lines"; it is Ellison's vision that all men, whether powerful or weak, are puppets controlled by invisible strings ("the force that pulls your strings"), like Clifton's dancing Sambo doll. Ellison's vision is of a complex chattering-monkey society composed of blind, mindless puppets wearing the masks assigned to them, playing the roles demanded of them, striking out blindly at the targets provided for them. A metaphor for this society is the battle royal ("suddenly alive in the dark with the horror of the battle royal"), in which the young black boys are set plunging and swinging wildly about a boxing ring. Blindfolded, they fight "hysterically," in a "confused" state of "terror" and "hate," while not one blow reaches the southern whites who are the makers of their pain and confusion. Tatlock comes to believe in the game, as the vet doctor will later warn the invisible man not to do, comes to believe that by striking at his comrade, the youthful invisible man, he is striking at a representative of whites (by virtue of the invisible man's college scholarship). Ironically, one of the white men has to remind the invisible man that he is nothing but a "Sambo." ⟨. . .⟩

Ellison differs from the other writers ⟨. . .⟩ in that he envisions no unifying force at the center of the cosmos; where the others see a pattern of meaning on which to build what Ellison calls a "plan of living," Ellison sees only "chaos." The human problem then becomes how "to give pattern to the chaos which lives within the pattern" of the "certainties" upon which blind men have built their societies. In *Symbolism and American Literature* Charles Feidelson calls Poe's philosophy "materialistic idealism." Allowing for the same possibility of a contradiction in terms, Ellison's philosophy might be called existential transcendentalism.

Richard Finholt, "Ellison's Chattering-Monkey Blues," *American Visionary Fiction: Mad Metaphysics as Salvation Psychology* (Port Washington, NY: Kennikat Press, 1978), pp. 98–100

---

**ROBERT G. O'MEALLY**        Ellison's political and critical positions have won him considerable animosity from whites and blacks alike. He maintains that art has functions that embrace the political but that differ from the rhetoric and cant of most political testimony. Ellison's truth is that of the artist; he insists upon the variety, ambiguity, comedy, tragedy, and terror of human life—beyond all considerations of political platforms. As a writer, Ellison's challenge is to charge one's work with as much life and truth as possible. Art, he says, is fundamentally a celebration of human life; it is not a wailing complaint about social wrongs.

This loftiness has not meant that Ellison has lost sight of his beginnings. Quite the contrary. Since his first review was printed in 1937, he has called for precise, sympathetic writing about the true nature of Afro-American experience. Never having written any fiction in which blacks do not figure centrally, Ellison has sought to capture in fiction the language and lore, the rites and the values, the laughter and the sufferings, as well as the downright craziness, which characterize black life in America. Ellison knows that the only way to grasp universal values and patterns is by holding fast to particularities of time, place, culture, and race. The Invisible Man is an identifiably Afro-American creature whose experience, nonetheless, is so deeply *human* that readers throughout the world identify and sympathise with him. ⟨. . .⟩

Ralph Ellison is a progressive and accomplished writer and intellectual, an American "man of good hope" in the tradition of Emerson, Mark Twain, Du Bois, and James Weldon Johnson. His importance lies in his unsinkable optimism concerning his race, his nation, man's fate. Moreover, it lies in his insistence on literary craft under the pressure of inspiration as the best means of transforming everyday experience, talk, and lore into literature.

Robert G. O'Meally, *The Craft of Ralph Ellison* (Cambridge, MA: Harvard University Press, 1980), pp. 180–81

---

**LOUIS MENAND**     *Going to the Territory* is filled with the stories of men and women who personify the kind of cultural mobility Ellison takes to be definitive of the American experience—a kind of mobility unknown to the world of *Native Son*. Among the book's heroes are Duke Ellington, whose music moves one, says Ellison, "to wonder at the mysterious, unanalyzed character of the Negro American—and at the white American's inescapable Negro-ness"; Romare Bearden, who is admired for discovering a method of painting that allowed him "to express the tragic predicament of his people without violating his passionate dedication to art as a fundamental and transcendent agency for confronting and revealing the world"; Inman Page, the first black to graduate from Brown and the principal of Ellison's segregated high school in Oklahoma City, who carried the culture of the Ivy League to the frontier; a music teacher—Hazel Harrison—at Tuskegee Institute in the 1930s who kept a signed Prokofiev manuscript on the lid of her piano; a black custodian with the extraordinary name of Jefferson Davis Randolph, at the Oklahoma State Law Library, whose advice white legislators sought out when they needed information on some point of law; and Richard Wright himself, who is celebrated in a short memorial sketch.

And there is a large cast of anonymous characters: the slaves who imitated and transformed the European dance steps they saw being performed through the plantation house window; the black workingmen who became sophisticated critics of grand opera by moonlighting as spear-carriers at the Metropolitan Opera House in New York; middle-class white kids who try to sound like a Baptist choir; even "the white youngster who, with a transistor radio, screaming a Stevie Wonder tune, glued to his ear, shouts racial epithets at black youngsters trying to swim at a public beach." But the chief figure in these essays, as it is in virtually everything Ellison has written since *Invisible Man*, is the young man who began his literary education at an all-black college in Alabama by looking up the books listed in the footnotes to *The Waste Land* and who eventually became the author of a best-selling novel— the figure of Ralph Ellison himself.

It is difficult to think of another writer—Wordsworth is the sort of person who comes to mind—who makes his own experience the touchstone for everything in as explicit and consistent a fashion as Ellison does. He regards the details of his own life—details that might seem to others exceptional or fortuitous—as emblems of general significance. He has transformed his biography, through many retellings, into a kind of parable of cultural possibility. The parable is offered in all humility, for it is Ellison's great virtue that he is unable to imagine that other people might be less capable of achievement than himself. Some virtues have a way of turning into handicaps, though, and it is also possible to feel that an inability to imagine lives more severely deprived of opportunity and determination can be Ellison's most serious shortcoming.

Louis Menand, "Literature and Liberation," *New Republic*, 4 August 1986, pp. 37–38

---

**KERRY McSWEENEY**     The big questions for the American novelist, as Ellison eloquently phrased them in 1957, were these:

> How does one in the novel (the novel which is a work of art and
> not a disguised piece of sociology) persuade the American reader
> to identify that which is basic in man beyond all differences of
> class, race, wealth, or formal education? . . . How does one
> persuade readers with the least knowledge of literature to
> recognize the broader values implicit in their lives? How, in a
> word, do we affirm that which *is* stable in human life beyond all

despite all processes of social change? How give the reader that
which we do have in abundance, all the countless untold and
wonderful variations on the themes of identity and freedom and
necessity, love and death, and with all the mystery of personality
undergoing its endless metamorphosis?

There is nothing new about these criteria for assessing a novel, nor about
Ellison's ambitions as a writer of prose fiction. Both are squarely in the great
moralizing tradition of the realistic novel. Ellison's claims, for example, are
essentially the same as those made by George Eliot in England in the middle
of the nineteenth century when she spoke of "the greatest benefit we owe
the artist [being] the extension of our sympathies. Appeals founded on
generalizations and statistics [i.e., on sociology] require a sympathy ready
made, a moral sentiment already in activity; but a picture of human life
such as a great artist can give, surprises [readers] into that attention to what
is apart from themselves, which may be called the raw material of moral
sentiment. [Art] is a mode of amplifying experience." In realizing their
intentions, both the author of *Invisible Man* and the author of *Middlemarch*
use the same general strategy of blending their directly expressed thematic
concerns and moral propositions with a densely textured, solidly specified,
and vividly presented social world. Many are the variations played in *Invisible
Man* on the themes of identity, freedom, and the mystery of personality;
but they are no less central to the novel than is the manifold of wonderfully
rendered aural and visual particulars: for example, the voices of Trueblood
recalling his sweet nights in Mobile, Peter Wheatstraw singing about his
woman, and Ras exhorting a mob; or the descriptions of the types who
frequent the lobby of the Men's House, of the crowd at Tod Clifton's funeral,
and of the clutter of household objects of the dispossessed couple, including
the paragraph-long description of the spilled contents of a single drawer
that the narrator picks up from the snow.

While the mixture of moral concern and felt life in *Invisible Man* is
traditional, the formal means employed to shape and organize the material
are modernist. In the artistic elaboration and presentation of its subjects,
and in the degree of formal control employed, Ellison's novel has more in
common with Joyce's *Ulysses* than with Eliot's *Middlemarch*. These elabora-
tions include the patterns formed by recurring images, symbols, and motifs;
the polyphonic organization of chapters, some of which have a realistic or
narrative level; the changes from chapter to chapter (and even within a
single chapter) in style and presentational mode—from straightforwardly

representational to expressionistic and surrealistic; and the intermittent use of techniques of defamiliarization (like the eruption of Jack's glass eye) and other devices that complicate the reader's engagement with the text. ⟨. . .⟩ one may say that one of the most striking and original features of *Invisible Man* is the counterpoint between a compelling story that is in its own right startlingly and sometimes horrifyingly eventful (there are no battle royals, police shootings, or race riots in *Ulysses*) and the high degree of artistic elaboration, which repeatedly invites the reader to reflect rather than to react.

Kerry McSweeney, Invisible Man: Race and Identity (Boston: Twayne, 1988), pp. 11–13

---

**EDITH SCHOR**      In discussing his work in progress with John Hersey, Ellison mentioned several problems he has had in writing this novel. He was satisfied with the parts but not with the connections between the parts, a problem that had also prolonged the writing of *Invisible Man*. In this novel, working the connections out is more complicated because the story is told by more than one main voice. Initially Ellison tried first-person narration, then third-person narration. His decision to stay out of the narrative and let the people speak for themselves stems from his long-held appreciation of American vernacular speech as one of the enrichments of literature.

Another difficulty Ellison spoke of is the need to determine what can be implied and what must be rendered for American sensibilities formed from so many different sources and social divisions. A writer must provide the reader "with as much detail as is possible in terms of the visual *and* the aural *and* rhythmic—to allow him to involve himself." Writing out of an individual sense of American life leaves the writer with an uncertainty about the social values that can be taken for granted by particular artifacts, symbols, or allusions. The writer can only evoke "what is already there, implicitly in the reader's head: his sense of life."

Another complication in writing this novel is that its dramatic incidents move back and forth in time. Time present in the novel is the mid-fifties, but the story goes back into earlier experiences too, even to some of the childhood experiences of Hickman who is an elderly man in time present. It's a matter of the past being active in the present—or of the characters becoming aware of the manner in which the past operates in their present lives. The sense of the past with its "systems of values, beliefs, customs, and hopes for the future that have evolved through the history of the Republic provides a further medium of communication" and allows for "that brooding, questioning stance that is necessary for fiction." Of course with one of the characters a senator, this gets into general history and even broader implications. ⟨. . .⟩

Since the novel remains a work in progress, further comment on it as an entity can only be conjecture. In contrast to the published fragments, which can be evaluated on their own, the novel they would comprise at present is the province of the creator, not the critic.

> Edith Schor, *Visible Ellison: A Study of Ralph Ellison's Fiction* (Westport, CT: Green-wood Press, 1993), pp. 136–37

# ❖ *Bibliography*

*Invisible Man*. 1952.

*The Writer's Experience* (with Karl Shapiro). 1964.

*Shadow and Act*. 1964.

*The City in Crisis* (with Whitney M. Young, Jr., and Herbert Gans). 1967.

*Going to the Territory*. 1986.

# Chester Himes
## *1909–1984*

CHESTER BOMAR HIMES was born in Jefferson City, Missouri, on July 29, 1909. His parents, Joseph and Estelle Bomar Himes, were both teachers. The family lived in several cities in the southern and midwestern United States, finally settling in Ohio. Himes graduated from Glenville High School in Cleveland in 1926 and studied for less than a year at Ohio State University before withdrawing, as his schoolwork was suffering because of his frequent carousing, gambling, and associating with pimps and criminals. In December 1928 he was convicted of armed robbery and sentenced to twenty years' hard labor in the Ohio State Penitentiary. He served seven years. During his incarceration Himes wrote many works of fiction, including a story based upon a tragic fire that broke out in the prison and killed 300 men. These tales began appearing in various magazines, including such black weekly newspapers as the *Atlanta World* and the *Baltimore Afro-American*.

Some time after his release in 1936 Himes joined the Ohio Writers' Project and went on to become a feature writer for the Cleveland *Daily News*. He was also involved with the labor movement and the Communist party. He married Jean Johnson in 1937. In 1942 Himes moved to California, where he worked at a variety of odd jobs in shipyards in Los Angeles and San Francisco. When he received a Rosenwald Foundation Fellowship in 1944, he moved to New York City to write. His first published novel, *If He Hollers Let Him Go* (1945), is a grimly realistic tale drawing upon his shipyard experiences. His first five novels were explosive studies of the situation of the black man in a racist society. They feature a considerable amount of autobiography, such as *Cast the First Stone* (1952), a story of prison life. These novels enjoyed only moderate success in America, and brought in such a small income that Himes was forced to work at a number of menial jobs to support himself. He separated from his wife in 1951 and later divorced her. When he noticed that he was being hailed in Europe as a powerful voice of social criticism, Himes decided to emigrate. He moved to the island of Majorca in 1954 and spent the rest of his life there and in Paris.

Himes was persuaded by the editor of the publishing house Gallimard to write detective novels for its crime series, La Série Noire. The result was his famous Harlem thrillers, such as *For Love of Imabelle* (1957), *The Real Cool Killers* (1959), and *The Heat's On* (1966). Many of these novels appeared in French translations before being published in English. One of them, *La Reine des pommes* (1958; an expanded version of *For Love of Imabelle*), won the Grand Prix Policier in 1958. Most of these works feature two black police detectives, Grave Digger Jones and Coffin Ed Johnson, and are characterized by fast-paced action and much violence. Himes occasionally returned to the protest vein of his early works, as in the mordant satire *Pinktoes* (1961) and his two volumes of autobiography, *The Quality of Hurt* (1972) and *My Life of Absurdity* (1976).

In the late 1950s and early 1960s Himes was romantically involved with a German woman, Marlene Behrens; sometime later he married an Englishwoman, Lesley Packard, with whom he remained until his death in Moraira, Spain, of Parkinson's disease on November 12, 1984. His *Collected Stories* appeared in 1990. His unfinished novel *Plan B* was published in a French translation in 1983 and in English in 1993.

# ▨ *Critical Extracts*

**HENRY F. WINSLOW**        The hero and narrator of *Cast the First Stone* is James Monroe, whose sentence of twenty years for robbery is understood to be a raw deal representing "exemplary justice." Monroe's narrative moves him over every conceivable department of his prison, mainly by means of transfers. The resulting pictures are revolting. For out of them issues the convincing charge that the life of the contemporary convict is so burdened with "prescribed routine and harsh discipline and grinding monotony" that only a wretchedness worse than death can come of it. His activity is without purpose, his glimmer of hope, the far-off possibility of freedom, and his days an unwinding eternity shadowed by "the constant sense of power just above, the ever present breath of sudden death," and the treacherous temptation of sexual perversion in the absence of women. ⟨. . .⟩

The last one hundred pages of *Cast the First Stone* tell a weird but focused story of a "love affair" between Monroe and Dido. It is here that prison-bred madness is shown to have fed upon itself to the point of bursting in repulsive degeneracy. The hero puts it thus: "But in that place of abnormality of body and mind there was something about his love for me that seemed to transcend degeneracy and even attained, perhaps, a touch of sacredness." Never was there a more justifiable fate than that which comes to the pathetic creation that was Dido.

Henry F. Winslow, "Sustained Agony," Crisis 52, No. 12 (December 1945): 246–47

---

**RICHARD WRIGHT**      Jerky in pace, *If He Hollers Let Him Go* has been compared with the novels of James M. Cain, but there is more honest passion in 20 pages of Himes than in the whole of Cain. Tough-minded Himes has no illusions: I doubt if he ever had any. He sees too clearly to be fooled by the symbolic guises in which Negro behavior tries to hide, and he traces the transformation by which sex is expressed in equations of race pride, murder in the language of personal redemption, and love in terms of hate.

To read Himes conventionally is to miss the significance of the (to coin a phrase) bio-social level of his writing. Bob Jones is so charged with elementary passion that he ceases to be a personality, and becomes a man reacting only with nerves, blood and motor responses.

Ironically, the several dreams that head each chapter do not really come off. Indeed, Himes's brutal prose is more authentically dreamlike than his consciously contrived dreams. And that is as it should be. In this, his first novel, Himes establishes himself not as what has been quaintly called a New Negro but as a new kind of writing man.

Richard Wright, "Two Novels of the Crushing of Men, One White, One Black" (1945), cited in Michel Fabre, Richard Wright: Books and Writers (Jackson: University Press of Mississippi, 1990), pp. 212–13

---

**STOYAN CHRISTOWE**      Chester Himes's new novel ⟨*Lonely Crusade*⟩ is a study of the American Negro, a brave and courageous probing into the Negro psyche. His diagnosis reveals a racial malady for which there is no immediate remedy. The cure, as he sees it, is centuries of equality and miscegenation. And in the beginning simple equality is not enough. Equality to the Negro means special privileges.

Mr. Himes's hero, Lee Gordon, is indeed a lonely crusader, seeking justice in a white ocean of prejudice and discrimination. A college graduate, a sensitive Negro of basic honesty and integrity, he comes up against the usual barriers. His college degree cannot get him a white-collar job, and since he refuses to take menial work, he and his devoted wife live in poverty, with the result that Lee Gordon's sense of manhood and fitness is gradually corroded, and his wife loses faith in him, though not her love for him. This tragedy Lee Gordon blames on the white man. ⟨. . .⟩

Hatred reeks through his pages like yellow bile. The Negro hates the Jew and the Gentile and he hates his own Negroness; the Jew hates the Negro and the Gentile and his own Jewishness. The pure Marxist Rosenberg, who hates nobody except the capitalists, is expelled from the Communist Party because of his goodness.

The strict Party-line Communists will not like Mr. Himes's book and will no doubt denounce it. The Trotskyites will probably take it to their bosoms, as certainly will all those who believe in unions free of Communist control. As for the Negro problem, it occasionally finds momentary resolution in oversexed white women mixing up Marxism with Negro macrogenitalism.

Stoyan Christowe, [Review of *Lonely Crusade*], *Atlantic Monthly* 180, No. 4 (October 1947): 138

**LeROI JONES**      If you think of W. E. B. Du Bois, Richard Wright, Jean Toomer, Langston Hughes, Ellison, Baldwin, Chester Himes and all the others, if you think of these people you are forced to realize that they gave a top-level performance in the areas in which each functioned. The most meaningful book of social essays in the last decade is *Notes of a Native Son,* by Baldwin. The most finely constructed archetypal, mythological novel, utilizing perhaps a Kafkaesque sense of what the world really has become, is *Invisible Man,* by Ralph Ellison. The most completely valid social novels and social criticisms of South and North, non-urban and urban Negro life, are Wright's *Black Boy* and *Native Son.*

It's all there, even to the Raymond Chandler–Dashiell Hammett genre of the detective novel, in Chester Himes' *All Shot Up* or *The Crazy Kill* or *The Real Cool Killers* which are much more interesting, not only in regard to plot but also in terms of "place," a place wherein such a plot can find a natural existence. So that the Negro writer finally doesn't have to think about his "roots" even literarily, as being subject to some kind of derogatory statement—one has only to read the literature.

> LeRoi Jones, "Philistinism and the Negro Writer," *Anger, and Beyond: The Negro Writer in the United States*, ed. Herbert Hill (New York: Harper & Row, 1966), pp. 58–59

---

**EDWARD MARGOLIES**     What Himes seems to draw mainly from his American background—middle class, working class, *lumpen* lower class and criminal years—is that the one central fact of the black man's life in America is violence. His two black police detective heroes, the dangerously hot-tempered Grave Digger Jones and Coffin Ed Johnson, are modelled, he says, on a couple of black policemen he knew in Watts, one of whom shot the other for seducing his wife. As regards scenes in his novels in which throttled, mauled, sliced, whipped, stabbed, garroted victims of violence who themselves have committed similar kinds of violence on others, thrash blindly about—these, Himes claims, are drawn as much from what he has seen and known of black life in America, in and out of prison, as from his imagination. Thus Himes, despite the slapstick and sometimes surreal quality of his work ⟨. . .⟩, speaks from the "inside"—that is, speaks from experience in a way that no other American writer of crime fiction has been able to do since Dashiell Hammett who was himself a former Pinkerton agent. Indeed in this regard Himes has greater claim, since Hammett knew best the world of the pursuer in the pay of established if not always upright authorities whereas Himes' milieu was ⟨. . .⟩ the underworld itself.

> Edward Margolies, "The Thrillers of Chester Himes," *Studies in Black Literature* 1, No. 2 (Summer 1970): 2

---

**CHESTER HIMES**     I have always believed—and this was from the time that *If He Hollers* . . . was published—that the Black man in America should mount a serious revolution and this revolution should employ a massive, extreme violence. This is based on the assumption Black people want to do it. I believe that this would change the conditions of the Black man in America, if he would mount a violent revolution in the West; that would be of benefit to two-three million people. If the Black man would mount a revolution that would result in the death of three million people— even if most, or at least two-thirds, were Black people themselves, it would still change the position of the Black man in America or in the world. Because I believe the Black man in America holds the destiny of the entire Western world. He holds the destiny in his hands because a study of the economy of the world will show you that if America fails as a nation then all the white Western world will fail, and the Eastern world will move in and take over. If this ever happens, which I don't think is possible, but if they did mount a revolution in force, then all the institutions would collapse. The economy of America would be the first to collapse. The American dollar—even in the series of riots which happened a couple years ago—the dollar slid on the world market; the people lost confidence in the whole American economy, and all the nations in the world were getting ready to jump away from America and let it sink. America is the nation that keeps the Western world alive economically. So once the institutions and the economic system in America fails, the Blacks are going to fail. But if they use this extraordinary power, they must not be deterred by the white community sheltering them. Because the white community has worked out a very thorough system in which they will play with the Black community. . . . This is a game played with intricate skill. If the Blacks would reject that game altogether—reject the whole idea—just say they're tired of the game, we don't want you doing it, and then move in force against the entire white structure, then America, to save its economic structure, its capitalistic structure, will give anybody anything. They'll give the Black man his equality and everything else to save the American way of life and economic structure in the world. They'll make these concessions and do anything. They're doing it now. They're trying to find out how they can do it without suffering any damage to their economic system. They're ready right now to ship the South Vietnamese out and gobble anybody else. There's no ideology involved in the American movements in the world. They're just trying to protect themselves and trying to protect their way of life, and if it is challenged, the only people who can challenge it thoroughly are the Blacks themselves.

Chester Himes, cited in Hoyt W. Fuller, "Traveler on the Long, Rough, Lonely Old Road: An Interview with Chester Himes," *Black World* 21, No. 5 (March 1972): 18–19

**ISHMAEL REED**        Of course a writer who has sweated over millions of words is bound to make some bloopers and Himes has his share of ouches, and flops, repetitions, speechiness, plots that start out strong and fizzle; that's probably why some people call it quits after two books. But Himes wouldn't be Himes if he didn't continue striking. ⟨. . .⟩

The fact that after two excellent novels Chester Himes was compelled to work as a porter and caretaker, and after four novels, pawn his jewelry, tape recorder, and typewriter is an ignominy in an industry that prides itself as standard bearer of all that is realistic and good about western civilization. The piddling advances, the racist distribution and promotional policies, the sleazy covers, and dumb jacket copy (see the foul, lurid, irresponsible third paragraph printed in bold type on the first page of Signet's *Cast the First Stone* under corny head, "James Monroe Was A Cool Cat") which afflicted Himes' career make the promotional abilities of his publishers seem a step above those of the man who hawks hotdogs at the football game. (At least he doesn't sabotage his product by packaging it in poison.) ⟨. . .⟩

Despite the setbacks, the sheer hatred directed at him by everybody, it almost seems, Himes has carried on. One has the feeling that had he remained in United States he would have been destroyed by whites, and by Blacks, some of whom will proclaim their Blackness to any available listener, yet seem so destructive about the best of their own culture. ⟨. . .⟩

I believe that it will be left to a young generation of Black and white critics to assess the importance of Chester Himes as a major twentieth century writer. "Serious" works, *Lonely Crusade, If He Hollers Let Him Go, Cast the First Stone, The Third Generation, The Primitive, Pinktoes,* etc., are of such high quality that their worth is only resisted by critics who have little interest in writing, a near pathological contempt for writers, and only care about evangelizing for some particular ideology. Europe freaks, Black and white have long denigrated the detective novel, probably because it is an American invention (Edgar Allan Poe); but things are changing. Nowadays people pride themselves on how much Chandler, Himes, Hammett, and Cain they know. Ross MacDonald's *The Underground Man* escaped the cloak and dagger sections of the book review and was praised up front. It won't be long before Himes' "Harlem domestic series," now dismissed by jerks as "potboiler," will receive the praise they deserve. ⟨. . .⟩

Many major Black writers have been influenced by Himes, whether by consciously using techniques Himes used earlier or by using similar story lines, characterizations, point-of-view, setting, and action. Episodes which occurred during Himes' visit to Paris have been dramatized in John A. Williams' great suspense novel, *The Man Who Cried I Am*. The scenery and action which occurred at a southern college in *The Third Generation*, the communist party's suspicions concerning Lee Gordon, the Black agitator in *Lonely Crusade*, are similar to scenes and actions in Ralph Ellison's *Invisible Man*. The way both authors approach these scenes and situations is a difference in style.

Ishmael Reed, "Chester Himes: Writer," *Black World* 21, No. 5 (March 1972): 37–38, 83–84

**RAYMOND NELSON**    Himes never becomes sentimental about Harlem; he permits himself no unrelieved nostalgia. The most prominent characteristics of the community that he chronicles are fear and brutality. His Harlem is an isolated world motivated and ordered by violence. The novels themselves are in a sense his violent assaults upon the reader. Himes is a fighter, a sort of literary Muhammad Ali (or, perhaps more accurately, Jack Johnson), and he writes with the same intense ferocity with which he might knock a man down. As he told John A. Williams—and the remark can be applied to the method as well as the theme of his series—"After all, Americans live by violence, and violence achieves—regardless of what anyone says, regardless of the distaste of the white community—its own ends." This emphasis on violence as a means—a revolutionary tactic, a method of survival, a mode of communication—helps to explain the troubling brutality with which the profoundly decent Coffin Ed and Grave Digger conduct their investigations. It is the only means at their disposal. They work within a system as closed as those electrical circuits that operate from a power-source since removed from the circuit itself—the works are set going but the first mover is withdrawn. Each problem the detectives face has its origin in the forbidden white city that surrounds Harlem. When Coffin Ed and Grave Digger confront criminal disorder they are thus limited to symptoms; the actual malfunction is inaccessible. Harlem problems are violent; they can be fought locally, and the delicate balance of community life sustained, only by an even more uninhibited violence. It is one of the brilliant ironies of the Harlem Domestic stories that the detective-heroes can express their genuine love for their people, their altruistic hopes for communal peace and decency, only through the crude brutality that has become their bitter way of life.

Raymond Nelson, "Domestic Harlem: The Detective Fiction of Chester Himes," *Virginia Quarterly Review* 48, No. 2 (Spring 1972): 269–70

**STEPHEN F. MILLIKEN**      Himes is a black American, and inevitably—in spite of his own very different ambitions—the role of spokesman for the race was thrust upon him as a writer. Few categories could have suited him less, yet he could not put pen to paper without telling the story of his people, and, from the beginning, critics insisted on judging his writing, to his own immense disgust, solely on its value as "protest." In addition to its special provinces, Himes's work treats—and this is true too of all the important black American writers—every aspect of the human condition, the complete plight of twentieth-century man. The harsh issues of race and racism in Himes's work are immensely important, but they are very far from being the only issues treated. Every fully committed writer is of one time and one people, but also of all times and all people, and there can be no question as to the completeness of Himes's commitment. ⟨. . .⟩

The bitter laugh of the dedicated satirist runs through much of Himes's work, but nowhere is there to be found the limpid moral certainty of the greatest satirists. And Himes's laughter is jubilant and gay as often as it is bitter.

His favorite subject was pain, and it screams in naked release on almost every page he has written, but justice, easily the most turgid and pompous of literary subjects, is invoked only slightly less often.

In his youth Himes served a long term in prison, and at times his writing has the glacial hardness that tends to characterize much of the work of those writers, from Dostoevski to Dalton Trumbo, who have been purged in that particular scale model of hell. Moreover, disturbing shadows of sadism flicker through many of Himes's lovingly detailed descriptions of violence. Yet it is always with the victim that this writer identifies, even when the victim is white and the assailant black. And he can be guilty of the most egregious sentimentalism wherever young lovers are involved.

Stephen F. Milliken, *Chester Himes: A Critical Appraisal* (Columbia: University of Missouri Press, 1976), pp. 2, 4–5

**A. ROBERT LEE**     *The Third Generation* (1954) acts as the diaristic record of a family's decline which works over a number of close autobiographical sources, now available in *The Quality of Hurt*. It lies near to Truman Capote's category of the non-fictional novel, personal history only lightly fictionalized. Crowded, at several points slack in laying out its heavy texture of detail—Himes was possibly too close to parts of the story—it maps out the dereliction of the Black bourgeois Taylor family, "Professor" Willie, his wife, and three sons. The Taylors take a downward journey from South to North involving dislocation which is a direct consequence of the mother's blighting pride in the lightness of her skin (she can pass) and the conviction that her white heritage confers a mark of racial specialness (it does, a victimizing mark), a reprimand to her husband's Black and artisan lowliness. The mother's implosions of anger and pain and their impact on her darker-skinned husband, a personable teacher of ironcraft, bequeaths to Charles, the youngest son, on whom the novel comes to focus—he is 18 in the late 1920s—a new set of embitterments. The family's sober picaresque travels from town to Southern town—Himes offers several excellent lyric vignettes of childhood—and their eventual migration into urban Cleveland give spatial definition to Charles' private awakenings and the parents' domestic storms. In the distant hinterland, touching the Taylor family only at margins, stands the Twenties' other face, the wealthier exuberance of Flapper and Jazz baby whose literary custodian was Scott Fitzgerald.

Of the Taylors as individuals, the father, deprived of his professional status on the Black campuses of the South, dies in a knifing. Tom, the eldest boy, drifts into obscurity. Charles, self-accusing, lonely, an artist manqué, drops out from college into the petty crime which puts him in prison and into the charge of the courts. The mother, for whom the legacies of color have reserved their most ingenious devising, slows down finally, a female Sutpen alone in the city who broods over her dynastic embers and fades sadly into senescence. Only William Lee, Jr., the son blinded in a gunpowder accident, finds an accommodation with his life. Like Himes' own blind brother he moves into academia. The cruel freak of blindness removes from his sight, at least, the disabling spectacles of segregation, the thrash of Lilian Taylor to de-negrify her family.

A. Robert Lee, "Violence Real and Imagined: The World of Chester Himes' Novels," *Negro American Literature Forum* 10, No. 1 (Spring 1976): 17

**LOYLE HAIRSTON**        My *Life of Absurdity* reveals how exile compelled the author to dissipate a fine intelligence, sensitivity and talent in
the drudgery of maintaining himself while he clawed and scratched his way
to some kind of success. But since acceptance and acclaim only come with
money success, what chance did an exiled Black writer of fiction have?
Even a good writer whose work didn't even sell in his own country. And
Chester Himes is a good writer with a creative mind and an incisive grasp
of the stresses that provoke tragic personality conflicts. *If He Hollers*, *The
Third Generation*, and *The Primitive* are novels that belong to the mainstream
of U.S. fiction as much as any American writer's work. In a less hypocritical
country he probably would have gotten the recognition he believed he
earned on the literary quality of his earlier work.

But America had no interest in entertaining Chester Himes' wishes. After
all, the country already had its celebrated Black novelist in Richard Wright;
and one at a time was the rule of the liberal game. So much for American
egalitarianism! Frustrated, dismayed, Himes fled to Europe. But since there
is little in My *Life of Absurdity* to show that he has recovered from the
"hurt" of America, he either fled too late in life or didn't flee far enough.
Unlike Richard Wright whose exile resulted from deep philosophical, psychological conflicts in a stifling anti-intellectual cultural atmosphere, Himes
fled for very different reasons. He went to Europe to achieve what America
had denied—recognition and success.

My *Life of Absurdity* is a deceptive book, though written simply and
without seemingly any prearranged attempt to make any specific points
about his life except as he lived it. On one level I found it difficult to take
Chester Himes seriously; became annoyed with his inanities and preoccupation with an endless stream of simple-minded incidents and banalities.
Written in the fast-paced style of a potboiler, the narrative is indeed a
novelized catalog of absurdities, some as vulgar as they are entertaining, as
pointless as they are amusing, as stupid as they are interesting. But on
another level I began to feel the bitterness underneath the lively, seemingly
light-hearted narrative, giving off an overall impact of documented despair.
This is the autobiography of a man disillusioned with his fellow creatures
and weary from the struggle to win acceptance from those he has grown to
despise. The problem, however, is that Himes has been consumed in the
process, though he achieved at least a measure of his ambition in the twilight
years of his life.

        Loyle Hairston, "Chester Himes—'Alien' in Exile," *Freedomways* 17, No. 1 (First
    Quarter 1977): 15–16

**JAMES SALLIS**      *Pinktoes*, published in 1961 by Olympia Press, and in the U.S. in 1965, is something of a sport. Though it introduces the boisterous comedy that became a signature of the Harlem novels and takes up yet again the author's disdain for the black middle class and fascination with interracial sex, there is nothing else like it in Himes' work. The success of *Candy* and other sexual farces somewhat earlier probably accounts both for this book's existence and considerable popularity. Centered around the activities of Harlem "hostess" Mamie Mason, who believes race relations (and her own social pretensions) best served in bed, *Pinktoes* is a scattergun that misses very few targets.

Most of the novel concerns one of Mamie's parties and its aftermath for two men there, black leader Wallace Wright and Art Wills, soon to become (white) editor for a Negro picture magazine. Plot turns and scenes grow ever more grotesque and outrageous. When Mamie, because Art will not feature her in his first issue, tells his wife that he has proposed to a black woman named Brown Sugar, the wife goes home to mother. Word quickly gets around that white liberal husbands are fleeing their wives for brownskin girls and there's a panicked run on suntan lotion and ultraviolet lights. A company that had been producing a skin lightener called "Black Nomore" prospers with its new product "Blackamoor." White women rush to kink their hair, dye their gums blue, redden their eyes.

The attacks are savage ones, true—and unrelenting—yet in the conscious self-parody of his own obsession with interracial sex, and in the unbridled lampoonery of all he held in contempt, Chester Himes seems to have found a kind of deliverance from the pervasive bitterness and gravity of previous work. Without *Pinktoes*, there could have been no Harlem novels, and possibly no more writing at all.

> James Sallis, "In America's Black Heartland: The Achievement of Chester Himes," *Western Humanities Review* 37, No. 3 (Autumn 1983): 203

---

**TRUDIER HARRIS**      In Chester Himes's *If He Hollers Let Him Go* (1945), Robert (Bob) Jones, the protagonist, works not only to overcome his fear of the white woman, but to destroy her in the process; both efforts become definitions of manhood and means of overcoming a fear of castration. ⟨. . .⟩

Himes's hero exudes more confidence than one would perhaps expect in a black male character in a fictional world set in the early 1940s. Bob goes from Cleveland to California and finds work in a shipyard. His physique is one reason for his confidence:

> When I came out to Los Angeles in the fall of '41, I felt fine about everything. Taller than the average man, six feet two, broad-shouldered, and conceited, I hadn't a worry. I knew I'd get along. If it had come down to a point where I had to hit a paddy I'd have hit him without any thought. I'd have busted him wide open because he was a paddy and needed busting.

The physique which induces such pride in him will provide part of the evidence which will make his guilt so easy to assert in the rape case, for how could some poor defenseless white thing, no matter how large, protect herself against this hulking brute? He may no longer be in the wilds of Africa, or in the illiteracy of slavery, but he is still on the rampage against the virtue of white females. As his body becomes a case against him in the series of events which lead to the accusation of rape, Bob is caught between attempts to efface himself and a simmering rage that he should be so facilely intimidated on his job.

Prior to the incident with the white woman, however, the racist atmosphere at the shipyard has rather quickly changed Bob's consistent good feelings about himself to ones in which his actions are undercut by a foreboding fear. Each morning he wakes to it seeping into his skull and spine, spreading to his groin "with an almost sexual torture," and settling in his stomach "like butterfly wings." He lives "scared, walled in, locked up." Every day is a fight, even when he is tired of fighting; every day is filled with some tension-ridden encounter with a white person. No wonder, then, Bob has such a difficult time on his job. The tension increases when he is promoted to "leaderman" of a "coloured gang": many of the whites believe that no black man should have such a job. Consequently, the ones who are superior to him never stop viewing him as an oddity they are forced to tolerate. The ship thus provides an ideal setting for the white woman to act out her little play with Bob and to call the mob of white shipyard workers to her rescue.

Trudier Harris, *Exorcising Blackness: Historical and Literary Lynching and Burning Rituals* (Bloomington: Indiana University Press, 1984), pp. 53–55

**MICHEL FABRE and ROBERT E. SKINNER** ⟨. . .⟩ it seems clear in retrospect that ⟨Himes⟩ had come to disbelieve the possibility of simple justice for American black people, just as he had become certain of the necessity of organized and armed black revolution to change the American system. In *Blind Man with a Pistol*, he artfully amplifies these beliefs in an alternative scenario where his normally unbeatable heroes are stopped in their tracks by forces so sinister, so deeply imbedded, that they cannot even see them. Himes's reduction of their status from knights-errant to rat exterminators at the conclusion of *Blind Man* is a far more powerful comment on the defeat of justice than his symbolic murder of them in the final existing scene of *Plan B*.

*Plan B* thus remains an incandescent parable of racial madness as well as a retrospective of American racial history. The book begins as a thriller, then races toward a horrible climax. One might characterize it as a black *Apocalypse Now*, and although things are quieter now than they were in the 1960s, Himes's vision still strikes the reader's heart and reminds one of the angry unrest that still lies beneath the exterior of American society. Here, his fundamental pessimism reaches a paroxistic dimension in which sexuality can only be bestial, violence ruthless, and racism absolute.

Michel Fabre and Robert E. Skinner, "Introduction," *Plan B* by Chester Himes (Jackson: University of Mississippi Press, 1993), pp. xxvi–xxvii

# ❖ *Bibliography*

*If He Hollers Let Him Go.* 1945.

*Lonely Crusade.* 1947.

*Cast the First Stone.* 1952.

*The Third Generation.* 1954.

*The Primitive.* 1955.

*For Love of Imabelle.* 1957, 1958 (French; as *La Reine des pommes*; tr. Minne Danzas), 1965 (as *A Rage in Harlem*).

*Il pleut des coups durs.* 1958 (French; tr. C. Wourgaft), 1959 (as *The Real Cool Killers*).

*Couché dans le pain.* 1959 (French; tr. J. Hérisson and Henri Robillot), 1959 (as *The Crazy Kill*).

*Dare-dare.* 1959 (French; tr. Pierre Verrier), 1966 (as *Run Man, Run*).

*Tout pour plaire.* 1959 (French; tr. Yves Malartic), 1960 (as *The Big Gold Dream*).

*Imbroglio negro.* 1960 (French; tr. J. Fillion), 1960 (as *All Shot Up*).

*Ne nous enervons pas!* 1961 (French; tr. J. Fillion), 1966 (as *The Heat's On*).

*Pinktoes.* 1961.

*Une Affaire de viol.* 1963 (French; tr. André Mathieu), 1980 (as *A Case of Rape*).

*Retour en Afrique.* 1964 (French; tr. Pierre Sergent), 1965 (as *Cotton Comes to Harlem*).

*Blind Man with a Pistol* ⟨*Hot Day, Hot Night*⟩. 1969.

*The Autobiography of Chester Himes, Volume I: The Quality of Hurt.* 1972.

*Black on Black: Baby Sister and Selected Writings.* 1973.

*The Autobiography of Chester Himes, Volume II: My Life of Absurdity.* 1976.

*Miotte.* 1977.

*Le Manteau de rêve.* Tr. Hélène Devaux-Minie. 1982.

*Plan B.* 1983 (French; tr. Hélène Devaux-Minie), 1993 (ed. Michel Fabre and Robert E. Skinner).

*Collected Stories.* 1990.

⊞ ⊞ ⊞

# John Oliver Killens
## *1916–1987*

JOHN OLIVER KILLENS was born on January 14, 1916, in Macon, Georgia. He was exposed from an early age to black American literature by his parents and by his schoolteachers, thereby gaining knowledge of traditional black mythology and folklore, which later appeared in his writings. He attended a variety of universities and law schools while working for the National Labor Relations Board (1936–42); but after serving in the U.S. Army during World War II as a member of the Pacific Amphibian Forces, he abandoned the idea of becoming a lawyer and concentrated on writing instead.

After the war Killens returned to his job with the Labor Board, but became increasingly cynical about the possibility of harmony between white and black workers. Around 1950 he formed an informal writing group (later to become the Harlem Writers Guild) where he read portions of his first novel, *Youngblood* (1954), dealing with the coming of age of Robby Young-blood in a Southern black family. It was generally well received, as was his second novel, *And Then We Heard the Thunder* (1962), about the treatment of black soldiers in the military. Killens drew upon his own experiences in the army for many of the details and incidents of this work, which was nominated for a Pulitzer Prize.

In the late 1950s Killens began work in film and theatre. He collaborated on the screenplay for the films *Odds against Tomorrow* (1959) and *Slaves* (1969), cowrote (with Loften Mitchell) the unpublished play *Ballad of the Winter Soldier* (1964), and wrote *Lower Than the Angels*, an unpublished play produced in New York in 1965.

Killens enunciated a number of his social and political positions in a collection of essays called *Black Man's Burden* (1965), in which he denounces nonviolent protest to racial oppression as ineffective. This position is illus-trated in *'Sippi* (1967), his third novel, concerning the issue of voting rights during the 1960s.

In *The Cotillion; or, One Good Bull Is Half the Herd* (1971) Killens attacks the black middle class, which, he claims, is disconnected from African heritage and identity. This novel was also nominated for a Pulitzer Prize, and he later adapted it for the stage. Killens also wrote two biographical sketches for children, *Great Gittin' Up Morning* (1975), about Denmark Vesey, the leader of a slave revolt, and *A Man Ain't Nothin' But a Man* (1975), about John Henry.

Killens was writer-in-residence at Fisk University (1965–68), Columbia University (1970–73), Bronx Community College (1979–81), and Medgar Evers College of the City University of New York (1981–87). He also served as vice president of the Black Academy of Arts and Letters and as a member of the executive board of the National Center of Afro-American Artists. He was married to Grace Ward Jones, and they had two children. John Oliver Killens died of cancer on October 27, 1987. A historical novel about Alexander Pushkin, *Great Black Russian*, based on travels to the Soviet Union in 1968 and 1970, was posthumously published in 1989. Another novel, *The Minister Primarily*, remains unpublished, as does a collection of essays on writing, *Write On! Notes from a Writers Workshop*.

# ▣ *Critical Extracts*

**HENRY F. WINSLOW**          Specifically, this keenly perceived novel ⟨*Youngblood*⟩ tells how Joe Youngblood and his wife Laurie Lee pitted their innate dignity and courage against Southern custom, and how the family was broken and the father destroyed for daring to assert their humanity. For Laurie Lee there is the poignantly presented, heart-breaking trial in which she chooses between lashing her son Robert for the sadistic appease-ment of southern law or seeing him committed to the total destruction of a "reformatory." For Joe there is the hard choice between dying a thousand times in galling humiliation or once for martyrdom. For their children there is troublous confusion. ⟨. . .⟩

Into this picture comes Oscar Jefferson, "the strangest cracker in Cross-roads," and his best friend Jim Collins, a sassy and aggressive Negro youth who grew up to become a labor organizer. It is Jefferson, however, who stands as the most memorable of Mr. Killens' characters, for through him Mr. Killens has illuminated one of the most misunderstood personalities in modern America: the tragic cracker. From his father, young Jefferson has learned to accept brutal thrashings; from his mother, a mixture of love and deception; from his friend Jim, the facts of life in race relations. The result is a serious-minded personality pondering the grave issues of right and wrong and finally realizing, in his slow, hesitant manner, that nearly all life as it is lived in the South is one huge complicated lie.

Also memorable in *Youngblood* is the authentic tone of its idiom. Mr. Killens' mastery of the language and thoughts of common folk makes the contrived diction of Amos and Andy very funny indeed. On the other hand, this novel reveals that the author has more film than focus. It could be many pages shorter even if the truthfulness of its subject matter argues against its being sweeter. Nevertheless, it proves that when a born storyteller has a clear understanding balanced between human nature and human society, the net effect makes for new light in August.

> Henry F. Winslow, "More Film Than Focus," *Crisis* 61, No. 8 (October 1954): 511–12, 515

---

**JOHN HOWARD GRIFFIN**      In this big, polyphonic, violent novel about Negro soldiers in World War II ⟨*And Then We Heard the Thunder*⟩, John Oliver Killens drags the reader into the fullness of the Negro's desolating experience. The author, formerly a member of the National Labor Relations Board in Washington and now a movie and television writer, served in the Amphibian Forces in the South Pacific. His novel, therefore, has the depth and complexity of lived experience. It calls James Jones to mind, though Killens writes with less technical control and more poetically. But his battle scenes have the same hallucinatory power; his characters live and speak the raw language of the streets and the barracks.

This non-Negro reader who served in the Pacific alongside Negro troops recognized the events and characters of this novel; but he sees them with a sort of brain-twisting transformation of insights. He never gave much thought, for example, to the hideous irony of asking the Negro to fight (in segregated units) and die in order to preserve the very freedoms which he could not enjoy at home. Few non-Negros knew the Negro soldier's common motto, the Double V for Victory: victory against Fascism overseas and victory against Fascism at home. Nor did it ruggle us to hear the band play "God Bless America" while we boarded troopships and then switch to "Darktown Strutters' Ball" when the Negro troops' turn came.

But here, living it through the Negro's reaction, we cannot believe our ears. We look up at the white soldiers on deck "waving and smiling inno-cently and friendly-like at the Negro soldiers below and yelling, 'Yeah, man!' and popping their pinky white fingers," and the same taste of gall creeps up from our stomachs into our mouths. And we hear a companion whisper, "We ain't no soldiers. We ain't nothing but a bunch of goddam clowns."

John Howard Griffin, "Color Line on the Front Line," *Saturday Review*, 26 January 1963, p. 46

---

**NELSON ALGREN**          Although the author ⟨in *And Then We Heard the Thunder*⟩ carries us through two years of warfare with a Jim Crow cast, complete with Cracker captain, he does not resolve the impossible predica-ment any more successfully than his hero. Yet he does reach for it:

"Perhaps the New World would come raging out of Africa and Asia," Saunders reflects, "with a new and different dialogue that was people-oriented. What other hope was there?"

Then he draws back. For while Mr. ⟨James⟩ Baldwin's report of oppression derives first-hand from the suffering of the American Negro, Mr. Killens' report rings more like a program to which he is a conscientious subscriber. His novel so lacks the feel and smell of barracks and of the passion of men at war that we remain unmoved, at the close, by Saunders' wistful wish "that whatever was left of the world would come to its senses and build something new and different and new and new and altogether different. He wanted to believe that East and West could meet somewhere sometime and sometime soon, before it was too late to meet."

This rings as rhetorically as the Jewish lieutenant announcing in the midst of gunfire, "I am a white man and I am your friend, and you are a Negro man and you are my best friend, and we are both friends of the human race." As Archie told Broadway-The-Lightning-Bug, "I don't hear no thunder."

Nelson Algren, "A Resolve to Do His Dancing at the Waldorf Yet Remember the Stompers at the Savoy," *New York Herald Tribune Books*, 14 April 1963, p. 8

---

**NAT HENTOFF**          ⟨. . .⟩ blacks continue to speak to whites, urging them at least to see and feel the American experience as a Negro. In *Black*

Man's Burden, novelist John Oliver Killens makes yet another attempt. In this short, blunt book, Killens, through fragments of autobiography and observations of the rising "mood ebony" among Negroes, speaks caustically not only of how unready white folks are for desegregation (let alone integration) but also of the increasing recognition among Negroes that there are pride and strength to be drawn from their history in this country.

Along with this pride goes an intensifying skepticism about absolute nonviolence. Now, except for a few black nationalists who talk actively of redemptive violence, the focus is, as with the "Deacons" in the South, on self-defense. But if basic change does not occur, Killens warns (and not just to frighten Whitey), there will be more explosions of hate and despair. One significant element in the upheaval in Los Angeles last summer was the attempt of some of the enraged quasi-colonials to break through the ghetto and bring the "rebellion" into white neighborhoods.

Although Killens is still talking to white America, his basic conclusion is: "We must make the Harlems of the U.S.A. sources of black strength, political and otherwise." That means motivating the masses of Negroes into an organized movement that will go beyond civil rights into political action—so that, as long as ghettos remain, their inhabitants will have decision-making power about their schools, housing and jobs. Much of the money for change will still have to come from Washington, but it will no longer be administered by outsiders.

Nat Hentoff, "Message for Whitey," *New York Times Book Review*, 27 February 1966, p. 14

---

**DAVID LITTLEJOHN**      James Oliver Killens has written two long, detailed, humorless, artless, almost documentary race novels, *Youngblood* (1954) and *And Then We Heard the Thunder* (1963). The first is a sort of Negro family epic, the expected tale of two generations of long-suffering blacks and their sadistic white masters in a Georgia town. The second tells the interminable story of Negroes (and whites) in wartime, where the ordeal of World War II seems less harrowing, in the long run, than the race war inside it. It runs through pages of somber "graphic realism," i.e., pages of vapidly obscene barracks chatter and hard-boiled crudeness of description: that's the way it was. Both books are sincerely well intended, and packed to bursting with details of Negro (Southern, army) life, episode after episode, as retailed by a careful, intelligent, unimaginative Negro with absolutely no sense of the art of fiction. They represent the kind of novel most Americans with great stocks of experience would probably write, if they had the will and were Negroes. The books are useful, and, to readers who make no great demands on their novelists, mildly moving and exciting.

David Littlejohn, *Black on White: A Critical Survey of Writing by American Negroes* (New York: Grossman Publishers, 1966), pp. 143–44

---

**RONALD WILLIAMS**      John Oliver Killens' *'Sippi* ⟨. . .⟩ has been heralded as his most ambitious novel. After reading all 434 pages of this novel, I decided that Mr. Killens' first line in this classically bad novel should have been "Once upon a time there was a fair, white, golden haired maiden who lived in the big house on the hill and a handsome, black boy who lived in a shack down in the valley on the girl's father's plantation." Everyone knows the story by heart. Naturally the golden-haired one and the little black boy are going to meet in the woods, the bedroom, the tree, the cave, or wherever, and fondle each other. Innocent sex play but in mixed hue. This is the beginning of what proves to be a series of deadly, plodding events that all lead nowhere. ⟨. . .⟩

All the characters move through *'Sippi* in two dimensional, sleepwalker's stupor saying things that are expected of them in light of the plot and message. They just don't come to life. These shadowy people are used as good propaganda foils. Now there is nothing wrong with this kind of polemic. It is not a novel. I find it impossible to say anymore about this novel. I do not object to the theme, the people, the locale. I find that it is not art. We know nothing more about the people, the situation, and the past or present than could be casually picked up from reading the *New York Times*.

Perhaps the fault is that there are too many writers who have not learned· that there is nothing so deadly as the stereotypical Southern racial conflict, Southern sexual dilemmas, and Southern myths. Whether white or black, these writers had better move beyond the history books, and the present psychological lore and tell us something about our dreams, nightmares, and partial consciousness. And in so doing engage our total being in this experience, as painful or joyous as it may be. To do less is not a sin; it just is not art.

Ronald Williams, [Review of *'Sippi*], *Negro Digest* 17, No. 1 (November 1967): 85–86

**GEORGE DAVIS**      *The Cotillion*, by John O. Killens, is a fast, beautiful, crazy novel, as crazy as a story told by a barbershop bullshitter; and thus it captures in the same way that some of our best contemporary Black Poetry does Black talk, Black rage, Black love, Black rhythm and wild Black exaggeration. It signifies and lies and intrudes on itself whenever it sees fit. It dances around while it is talking and comes all out of itself to make sure you get the point that it is making. It starts to exaggerate and keeps on exaggerating even though it knows that you know that the truth is being stretched out of shape.

In the barbershop you might say, "Man, you ought to quit that lying," while you're cracking up over the funny way the dude is telling the story.

Most novels make use of the sense of sight to draw the reader into the fictional universe, but this one sounds and feels like Harlem. ⟨. . .⟩

This novel is shorter than John Killens' earlier works. It moves faster toward its climax, which is a Grand Cotillion at the Waldorf for the daughters of the colored first families of Crown Heights, Brooklyn, and five culturally deprived Blacks from Yoruba's neighborhood in Harlem. ⟨ . . .⟩

The novel is written in Afro-Americanese, and it is full of the kind of street-corner sayings and jokes that an ethnologist might get a grant from the Library of Congress to come up to Harlem to record. But in 1971 we don't need any of that. We can put these things on record ourselves. This John Killens has begun to do.

George Davis, [Review of *The Cotillion; or, One Good Bull is Half the Herd*], *Black World* 20, No. 8 (June 1971): 51–52

**NICK AARON FORD**      His most important literary work is his second novel, *And Then We Heard the Thunder* (1963), the most significant treatment of the black American soldier in World War II. It is a story of a company of black soldiers, its unofficial leader Sergeant Solly Saunders of Harlem, its Jewish Lieutenant also from New York City, its white Captain from Texas, and three women who love the black sergeant. At first Sergeant Solly is proud of his role, for he is convinced that the war is for democracy at home and abroad. But when his segregated company arrives in Georgia to continue its training, the numerous incidents of humiliation and brutality inflicted by white fellow-soldiers destroy his illusions and he joins several comrades in a bitter letter of protest released to the Negro press. "Some of us feel," the letter stated, "that we do not need to go four or five thousand miles to do battle with the enemies of Democracy. They are present with us here and now and spitting in our faces . . . riding on our backs and breathing down our necks. God only knows why we haven't taken matters in our own hands, or when we might. . . ." ⟨. . .⟩

⟨. . .⟩ At the end the black sergeant has reached three major conclusions: (1) material success is intolerable without freedom and dignity; (2) whites are not yet willing to accept Negroes as equals, regardless of their education, talents, or achievements; (3) the white man's rejection of the Negro on terms of equality has resulted in a similar rejection of him by the Negro.

Nick Aaron Ford, *Black Insights: Significant Literature by Black Americans, 1760 to the Present* (Waltham, MA: Ginn & Co., 1971), p. 319

---

**JOHN OLIVER KILLENS**      I think I'm a man who has made a helluva lot of mistakes in my time, but I have always been in there pitching. I have always worked for Black liberation, but I've changed my mind a million times about how we're going to achieve it. For two years I was a CIO organizer. I had hopes that we could liberate the nation by joining hands with the white working class. Big mistake, but I learned from it. The thing is to learn from your mistakes. I was not disillusioned when the working class joined the KKK and voted for Wallace (I don't mean Henry). I wasn't disillusioned because I had no illusions in the first place. I just had high hopes. I was optimistic. When the labor movement didn't make it and was co-opted by the establishment, I said to myself, "Okay, that's that." I didn't really believe it anyhow. How could I? Growing up as I did in Macon, Georgia. I don't want to make a fetish or a religion out of mistake making. But I do insist on my right to make them if they're not too costly to me and my people, and also my right to change my mind, to change me. I am seldom able to conceal my discomfort when I bump into a brother or sister I haven't seen since *Youngblood* was published and the brother comes on strong with: "I been keeping up with you. And the thing I like about you, you haven't changed. You haven't changed!" I know the brothers mean a compliment but it never fails to throw me. It's like saying to me, "Man, you're the most dogmatic, stagnated, unchanging, foot-dragging, non-progressive motherfucker in the whole world!" What they really mean, of course, is my head has not become swollen by the sweet smell of so-called "success." But even that ain't hardly absolutely true. I am no noble savage. And no man has that much humility.

To be a creative artist is to have the capacity for change, for, I repeat, self-criticism. The capacity to admit mistakes openly but especially to yourself, and not to let them hang you up, immobilize you, make you cop out, feel sorry for yourself and all that shit, but learn from them and keep moving on up.

> John Oliver Killens, "Rappin' with Myself," *Amistad 2*, ed. John A. Williams and Charles F. Harris (New York: Random House, 1971), pp. 121–23

---

**WILLIAM H. WIGGINS, JR.**      ⟨. . .⟩ Killens has made the customary literary use of ⟨the⟩ folklore genre, i.e., he uses them to invoke some response from his readers, such as humor or to register social protest. In many of his folktales humor and social protest are combined. In *'Sippi* Killens breaks new literary ground for black novelists. In this novel he not only uses the message of a traditional folklore genre, but more importantly he uses the structural form of the folktale as a formal outline for his novel. Hence, it is not possible to remove the "Sippi" folktale from Killens' novel and have the same book. The novel *'Sippi* is really a longer and much more sophisticated offspring of her folktale father. ⟨. . .⟩

Killens skillfully develops the two major characteristics of this folktale: (1) the overt rejection of racial prejudice and (2) the affirmation of black manhood into a major novel. Black rejection of racial prejudice is present in all stages of black folklore, but in most instances the note of social protest has been more covert, e.g., the John Tales and many of the spirituals. But *'Sippi* is a new type of black folklore humor. Its message is much more biting than ⟨Richard M.⟩ Dorson's "protest humor." Words like "assertion" and "defiance" better capture the spirit of *'Sippi*. There is no tricking of John nor the innuendo of recently cited "integration humor." These two traditional means of expressing black discontent with white racism in America are absent from *'Sippi*. The humor in *'Sippi* is direct and to the nitty-gritty. It shouts to the white community: I ain't putting up with this racism no longer!

Mississippi is a racial metaphor in both the novel and the folktale. It embodies all of the hardships and racial indignities endured by black Americans during their stay in America. Present in this tale are degrading social customs, e.g., Negroes must enter by the back door; the superior status of the white man, and the tabooed white woman. All of these stifling social agents are openly rejected by the hero of this story; for him there will be no more time in which Mississippi intimidates the black man's assertion of his manhood. From now on there will be a new racial relationship between white and black men in America. This is not the age of Aquarius, but rather the age of '*Sippi*.

> William H. Wiggins, Jr., "Black Folktales in the Novels of John O. Killens," *Black Scholar* 3, No. 3 (November 1971): 55, 57

## ROSALIND K. GODDARD      John Oliver Killens, the noted black author, has resurrected Denmark Vesey from obscurity ⟨in *Great Gittin' Up Morning*⟩. In doing so he has also provided a social "profile" of 19th-century southern America. Because factual sources on Vesey's personal life are scarce, much, as Killens states in the foreword, is fictionalized in the early chapters of the book. ⟨. . .⟩

Killens attempts to portray Vesey as a heroic figure who, though more self-sufficient and well-read than most of his white peers, coolly and forcefully assaults the caste system which enslaved thousands of black men and women. There are scenes of Vesey challenging and debating whites openly and militantly; yet he is also shown as a gentle man fiercely loyal to family. We learn also of his uncompromising love for and sense of community with other blacks, free and enslaved. Finally, we see Denmark Vesey, the frustrated embittered black conspiring to destroy every white in the city of Charleston. ⟨. . .⟩

For all of its importance as a valid lesson in black history, though, the book falls short. In an effort to be true to the charisma of a revolutionary, Killens becomes overly dramatic and verbose. This detracts from Vesey's appeal as a human being. Killens overpowers the reader, sometimes with a profusion of adjectives or figurative statements that sensationalize the subject. ⟨. . .⟩ The drama of Vesey's heroism would have been better portrayed if the author's style had been more controlled and subtle.

> Rosalind K. Goddard, [Review of *Great Gittin' Up Morning: A Biography of Denmark Vesey*], *New York Times Book Review*, 30 April 1972, p. 8

**ADDISON GAYLE, JR.**     To categorize Killens by labeling him an integrationist or separatist is to understand neither the man nor his work. Go back to *Youngblood*, his first novel, and the major progression is in terms of form and structure. In content, subject matter, and emphasis, Killens has moved only a short distance, if at all, from his first novel. The overriding theme of each of his works is the coming out of his characters into black awareness, the discovery of their black heritage. That he was among the first of the contemporary novelists to write of proud black men and women has not been overlooked by those young writers, who realize that he was among the first to challenge the images and symbols prescribed by the manipulators of the word and the first to break with those championed by members of the Wright school.

More so than the people of Ralph Ellison, his are far removed from past and present stereotypes of Blacks. They are not the middle-class sycophants of old, nor the brainless revolutionaries of the present. They are such men as Bookworm Taylor, Quiet Man Larker, and Mathew Lovejoy, whose characters are delineated by the extent of their love and faith in black people. It is this love and faith the author has shared with his characters from *Youngblood* and *The Cotillion*. The Youngbloods, father and son, the Lovejoys, mother and daughter, Saunders and Lumumba all have this in common; they must be made conscious of their own strength and move to confront a changing world in the manner and style of their creative ancestors. They must move from a preoccupation with self to a preoccupation with the race in general, and they must come to realize that they possess a heritage as enduring and as ancient as the Nile. ⟨. . .⟩

One may score technical debating points against each of Killens' novels. If the plot sequence seemed too involved in *Youngblood* and *Thunder*, in *The Cotillion* it seems too slight to support a major satiric venture. Overwriting, a defect in the previous novels, is less in the latter, though some scenes and episodes are stretched out too long and others receive inadequate attention. Sentimentality, though minuscule in *The Cotillion*, mars the earlier novels, and Killens' difficulty with dialogue is corrected only in the latter work. To evaluate the novels based upon these defects, however, is to subtract from the richness of the works in terms of language and content, to ignore moving passages of prose in the earlier novels, and to ignore the diversity of black language styles utilized so expertly by the author of *The Cotillion*. The technical faults of Killens are those of exceptional novelists from Fielding to Kafka, and to point them out does not detract from Killens' substantial achievement in the novel form.

Addison Gayle, Jr., *The Way of the New World: The Black Novel in America* (Garden City, NY: Anchor Press/Doubleday, 1975), pp. 275–76

**NORMAN HARRIS**      The social backdrop of *The Cotillion or One Good Bull Is Half the Herd* is that part of the black power movement which advocated name changes, African attire, and other outward expressions of black conciousness as methods for Afro-Americans to exercise self-determination. Within this context, the novel explores the contradiction between appearance and reality by illustrating the interaction of Afro-American and Euro-American symbols. We see different members of the black community respond to the same set of symbols in glaringly different ways. As one might expect, the cotillion is the central symbol. In its purest state, the cotillion is presented as European, derived from eighteenth-century France. Yet, like so many European cultural expressions, once Afro-Americans "get hold" of them, their texture and flavor are dramatically altered. So, in one sense, the characters are in conflict as to how "black" a cotillion can be. More specifically, one group of characters is determined to have the black cotillion be as European as possible, whereas another group questions the extent to which the form itself (the cotillion) can be made to serve black needs.

Thus the major conflicts in the novel result from characters trying to balance the symbolic demands made by the black power movement with the demands made by their own personal histories. Those who run from any mention of Africa must shed an unattractive bourgeois veneer which is cracked and crumbling with age and, in a sense, be born again. Those who champion "Mother Africa" must move from their plateaus of symbolic correctness and merge with that which is good about black people regardless of their symbolic wrappings. They are faced with the task of obtaining freedom and literacy in an environment in which meanings associated with symbols constantly shift. ⟨. . .⟩

By shifting the point of view between the first, second, and third person, Killens manages to make the contradiction between appearance and reality very clear. Just when we are able to gauge the novel's point of view it shifts. The foreword is in the voice of the central character, Ben Ali Lumumba. He lets us know that the novel's structure, like the structured reality of black people, is an improvisation, a blending of different voices to create a functioning whole. Lumumba tells us that the novel will be a "Black, black comedy" meant to signify. "I [mean] to let it all hang out."

Although the black middle class as portrayed in the novel suffers most from this signifying, no segment of the black community—conservative, militant, or liberal—is spared. Signifying requires free movement and an associational expression that does not limit itself to clear categories based on generally accepted rules of discourse. Lumumba informs us: "Like I went to one of them downtown white workshops for a couple of months and got all screwed up with angles of narration, points of view, objectivity, universality, composition, author-intrusion, sentence structure, syntax, first person, second person. I got so screwed up I couldn't unwind myself for days. I said to hell with all that. I'm the first, second and third person my own damn self. And I will intrude, protrude, obtrude or exclude my point of view any time it suits my disposition." Having made explicit the contours of his poetic license, Lumumba indicates that they will be molded by "Black idiom, Black nuances, Black style. Black truths, Black exaggerations." The musical referent for the amalgamation is improvisational jazz—a fusion of several black musical traditions. The linguistic referent, according to Lumumba, is "Afro-Americanese, Black rhythm, baby." Improvisation informed by recurring rhythms dictated by a desire to "speak the truth" describes the method of Lumumba's signifying. This approach creates a point of view that defines itself in motion. *The Cotillion* thus appears as a novel always reaching toward literacy.

Norman Harris, *Connecting Times: The Sixties in Afro-American Fiction* (Jackson: University of Mississippi Press, 1988), pp. 140–41, 144–45

---

**CALVIN FORBES**     Posthumously published, John Oliver Killens's novel *Great Black Russian* is based on the life of Alexander Pushkin, considered by many one of the greatest poets—if not the greatest—of the Russian language. Pushkin's great-grandfather was African. The rest of his forebears were, to the best of my knowledge, "white" Russians. Does that make him black? It's an age-old question. ⟨. . .⟩

*Great Black Russian* is an old fashioned traditional novel, perhaps befittingly so, since Killens's is a voice from the era when a large detailed canvas was desired. It's a historical novel, and the early 19th century that Pushkin lived in was a swashbuckling time. Pushkin fought his share of duels over minute insults, and had more than a fair number of affairs, enough to earn him a reputation as a womanizer, as well as a skilled user of both pen and pistol.

Killens tells his story with suitable flair. Pushkin's adventures and troubled life (his mother thought him too dark and too inquisitive a child) are served up like a feast for us to enjoy.

Killens had a great deal of difficulty getting his novel published and didn't live to see it in print. Perhaps Killens's struggles ⟨. . .⟩ tell us something about the literary state in which writers of African descent live worldwide.

Calvin Forbes, [Review of *Great Black Russian*], *Washington Post Book World*, 4 March 1990, p. 8

# ▨ *Bibliography*

*Youngblood*. 1954.

*And Then We Heard the Thunder*. 1962.

*Black Man's Burden*. 1965.

*'Sippi*. 1967.

*Slaves*. 1969.

*The Cotillion; or, One Good Bull Is Half the Herd*. 1971.

*Great Gittin' Up Morning: A Biography of Denmark Vesey*. 1972.

*A Man Ain't Nothin But a Man: The Adventures of John Henry*. 1975.

*Black Man in the New China*. 1976.

*Great Black Russian: A Novel on the Life and Times of Alexander Pushkin*. 1989.

*Black Southern Voices: An Anthology of Fiction, Poetry, Drama, Nonfiction, and Critical Essays* (editor; with Jerry W. Ward, Jr.). 1992.

# Paule Marshall
## b. 1929

PAULE MARSHALL was born Paula Burke on April 9, 1929, the daughter of Samuel and Ada Burke. Her parents had emigrated from Barbados, and Paule grew up in West Indian neighborhoods in Brooklyn, New York. She kept close ties with Barbadian culture in both America and Barbados. She received a B.A. from Brooklyn College in 1953 and briefly pursued a master's degree at Hunter College while working as a librarian and a staff writer for *Our World* magazine. At the same time she began writing stories and articles for a variety of periodicals. She married Kenneth E. Marshall in 1950; they had one child and divorced in 1963.

Marshall's first novel, *Brown Girl, Brownstones* (1959), set in the West Indian neighborhoods of Brooklyn, tells of a young woman's struggle for identity in the West Indian subculture. Critics have characterized the novel as a *Bildungsroman* and compared it to Zora Neale Hurston's *Their Eyes Were Watching God*. It is marked by rich language, perhaps influenced by the oral traditions preserved in the West Indian community of her childhood, and sensitive character portrayal. The novel was a critical success but a commercial failure.

In 1960 Marshall was awarded a Guggenheim Fellowship to work on *Soul Clap Hands and Sing* (1961), her second book, a collection of tales bound generally by the theme of race. This volume, which won the Rosenthal Award from the National Institute of Arts and Letters, contains four long stories about African descendants in the United States, the Caribbean, and South America and their race relations with other immigrant groups. Marshall contrasts traditional African spiritual values with the commercialism and materialism of the New World.

Although Marshall received a Ford Foundation grant for 1964–65 and a National Endowment for the Arts grant for 1967–69, her next novel, *The Chosen Place, the Timeless People* did not appear until 1969. In this work Marshall examines, with the eye of an anthropologist, the changing society of a third-world Caribbean community as it emerges from under colonial rule.

In 1970 Marshall became a lecturer on creative writing at Yale University. She has served as guest lecturer at other universities, including Oxford, Columbia, Michigan State, and Cornell. In 1970 she married Nourry Menard. Her third novel, *Praisesong for the Widow* (1983), returns to the theme of the destructive power of materialism and exhibits Marshall's interest in mythology and historical memory. It won the Before Columbus Foundation Book Award in 1984. *Reena and Other Stories*, gathering tales written since 1962, also appeared in 1983.

Marshall's long-awaited fourth novel, *Daughters* (1991), is the complex tale of a New York woman of West Indian heritage struggling to come to terms both with racial tensions in the U.S. and with the family she left on a small island in the Caribbean. It too was generally well received by critics.

Marshall and her husband now live alternately in New York City and the West Indies.

# ◈ *Critical Extracts*

**CAROL FIELD**      Rarely has a first novel come to hand which has the poignant appeal and the fresh, fierce emotion of *Brown Girl, Brownstones*.

The "brown girl" of the book's title is Selina Boyce, daughter of Deighton and Silla, Negro immigrants from the island of Barbados. The "brownstones" are the once socially desirable houses in a section of Brooklyn, which this group has moved into. The story Mrs. Marshall tells so effectively is mainly about the Boyces, but touching their lives closely are a score of other characters who share their background and their problems.

Racial conflict and the anger and frustration it nurtures are part of this tale, but equally, if not more, important are the personal conflicts of men and women making roots in a new land, of men and women caught in duels of love and hate, of ambition, envy and failure. ⟨. . .⟩

This is an unforgettable novel written with pride and anger, with rebellion and tears. Rich in content and in cadences of the King's and "Bajun" English, it is the work of a highly gifted writer.

Carol Field, "Fresh, Fierce, and 'First,' " *New York Herald Tribune Book Review*, 16 August 1959, p. 5

**PHILIP BUTCHER**      Writing from the inside, from a short lifetime of experience, Paule Marshall achieves in *Brown Girl, Brownstones* (1959) a remarkably perceptive and mature story of a West Indian family's pursuit of happiness in Brooklyn. Selina, the heroine, is a sensitive child who admires above all else her indolent but charming father, Deighton Boyce. Her world is composed of her West Indian neighbors and the tenants in her home, including the inevitable prostitute and a very old white woman, Miss Mary, who lives with the ghosts of the aristocrats who walked in elegance behind the brownstone façade in the days when it was new. Deighton Boyce is even more of a dreamer than demented Miss Mary, but his visions are of the future. Undisturbed by a lifetime of failure, he is comforted by the illusion that he will someday build a white house on a bit of land he has inherited in his native Barbados. The prevailing obsession for security and respectability drives his wife to sell the land to relieve their poverty in Brooklyn, but Deighton takes his revenge by spending all the money on presents and clothes and a golden trumpet. Later he is converted to the cult of Father Divine. Even in heaven—Father Divine's heaven— the malice of his plodding wife pursues him. He is deported when she discloses that he has entered the country illegally. Within sight of Barbados, which means for him not home but public confession of failure, Deighton slips from his ship and drowns. Possibly at last he gains permanent entry into heaven, having known hell and purgatory largely of his own making.

With the passing years Selina becomes further estranged from her older sister, who finds fulfillment and respectability in the Espicopal Church, and from her mother, who obtains much the same values from the Association of Barbadian Homeowners and Business Men. The municipal college offers Selina partial escape from the narrow interests of the Barbadian community. Her release from the image of her father and her advance to womanhood are signalled by a love affair with a Barbadian bohemian, whose failure as a painter stems from his subjection by a possessive mother. Although she is an intelligent girl and a conscientious student, college means little to Selina except for the modern dance group, of which she is the only colored member. After a triumphant recital she is brutally reminded of her race by a malicious parent. She loses her spineless lover when she turns to him for consolation, but she gains a sense of identification with her Jewish girl friend, her mother, and the whole West Indian tradition. In her new maturity Selina accepts all that is best in her heritage but rejects the chauvinism, the provincialism, and the petty materialistic ambitions. Like other Barbadian girls, she has worn from birth two silver bangles. As she prepares to leave Brooklyn she hurls one of them into the night. The other remains on her arm.

Philip Butcher, "Younger Novelists and the Urban Negro," *CLA Journal* 4, No. 3 (March 1961): 201–2

**IHAB HASSAN**     Though her stories ⟨in *Soul Clap Hands and Sing*⟩ do not all claim America for a setting, Paule Marshall enriches our idea of Memory by gentle, lyrical brooding on the meaning of lives that have been already spent or shaped. Her four aged protagonists can neither clap nor sing. But they have some kindlings of rage, and the bitter dignity of knowledge through defeat. In this lies the unique quality of the book. ⟨. . .⟩

By far the best story is the last, "Brazil," a sharp yet moving account of a famous comedian about to retire. "O Grande Caliban," as everyone knows him (his true name and his identity seem lost forever), is Rio's implacable jester. A tiny man, he seems all his life a "Lilliputian in a kingdom of giants." "The world had been scaled without him in mind—and his rage and contempt for it and for those who belonged was always just behind his smile, in the vain, superior lift of his head, in his every gesture." Caliban's frenzied effort to reclaim his identity from the posters and cheering crowds, from the stupid, spoiled, blonde Amazon who is his partner, and even from his young, pregnant wife, takes him to the center of his personality and the terrifying slums of Rio. Here all is done with tact and great power.

The example of Caliban shows that an aged man may not be entirely a paltry thing. (Indeed, the sequence of stories in the book reveals a progressive vitality in the characters.) Paule Marshall does not bring new resources of form or startling sensibility to the genre. But she allows her poetic style to be molded in each case by the facts of her fiction; she has escaped the clichés that must doubly tempt every Negro author writing today; and she has given us a vision, precise and compassionate, of solitary lives that yet participate in the rich, shifting backgrounds of cultures near and remote. Her retrospective vision is really a forecast of what we may wake up, too late, to see. There is a need for a poetics of gerontology.

Ihab Hassan, "A Circle of Loneliness," *Saturday Review*, 16 September 1961, p. 30

**EDWARD BRAITHWAITE**    Anglophone West Indian literature—certainly its novels—has been mainly concerned with two main
themes: the relationship of the author's *persona* or *personae* to his society,
found in general to be limiting and frustrating; and stemming from this, a
presentation of that society and an illustration of its lack of identity. West
Indian novelists have so far, on the whole, attempted to see their society
neither in the larger context of Third World underdevelopment, nor, with
the exception of Vic Reid, in relation to communal history. Perhaps this
has been artistically unnecessary. West Indian novels have been so richly
home centered, that they have provided their own universe, with its own
universal application. West Indian novelists, faced with the exciting if
Sisyphean task of describing their own society in their own terms, for the
first time, have had to provide for themselves a priority list in which, quite
naturally, a relating of their own encounter with their environment, society
and sensibility, has had to take pride of place. In addition, since most West
Indian novelists have become exiles in several centres of the metropolitan
West, their concern with a continuing and widening exploration of the
societies has been limited by distance, separation and the concerns of a
different milieu. They have, most of them, continued to write about the
West Indies, but a West Indies stopped in time at the snapshot moment of
departure.

The question, however, remains as to whether the West Indies, or anywhere else for that matter, can be fully and properly seen unless within a wider
framework of external impingements or internal change. The contemporary
West Indies, after all, are not simply excolonial territories; they are underdeveloped islands moving into the orbit of North American cultural and
material imperialism, retaining stubborn vestiges of their Eurocolonial past
(mainly among the elite), and active memories of Africa and slavery (mainly
among the folk). ⟨. . .⟩

This way of looking at West Indian writing has been prompted by a
reading of Paule Marshall's new novel, *The Chosen Place, the Timeless People*.
Had Paule Marshall been a West Indian, she probably would not have
written this book. Had she not been an Afro-American of West Indian
parentage, she possibly could not have written it either; for in it we find a
West Indies facing the metropolitan West on the one hand, and clinging
to a memorial past on the other. Within this matrix, she formulates her
enquiry into identity and change. And it is no mere externalized or exotic
investigation. Mrs. Marshall has reached as far into West Indian society as

her imagination, observation, and memory will allow. The questions raised
and the answers suggested are, one feels, an integral part of her own development while being at the same—and for the first—time, a significant contribution to the literature of the West Indies.

The scope and value of this contribution is no accident. Paule Marshall's
background has prepared and qualified her for it. Born of Barbadian parents
in Brooklyn, she was brought up in a West Indian/Afro-American environment in New York which she explored in her first novel, *Brown Girl,
Brownstones* (1959). Visits to the West Indies, and especially ancestral
Barbados, revived and strengthened direct links with the Caribbean, as
many of her stories illustrate, including one in *Soul Clap Hands and Sing*
(1961). Now in *The Chosen Place, the Timeless People*, (1969), we have her
first mature statement on the islands—or more precisely, on a tiny, hilly
corner of Barbados she calls Bournehills (though there is Port-of-Spain
during Carnival and something of the Maroons of Jamaica as well).

Edward Braithwaite, "West Indian History and Society in the Art of Paule Marshall's
Novel," *Journal of Black Studies* 1, No. 2 (December 1970): 225–27

---

**LEELA KAPAI**     *The Chosen Place . . .* weaves in the race issue subtly
in the entire story. Harriet represents the spirit of the white world. She is
only a step ahead of the Bentons of this world. When she fails to comprehend
why a woman would sell the eggs to someone else rather than feed her own
family, she takes it to be another backward streak of the incorrigibles. Her
impotent anger and frustration come out vivid in the carnival scene where
she realizes that the reign of people like her is over and a new generation
is emerging. Her death seems to be a symbolic end of all that white America
stands for and the ever-mourning waves of the ocean perform the ablution
of the old sins of the past. Perhaps a new race of active men like Saul and
sympathetic ones like Allen will create better understanding between the
races.

This new world, Miss Marshall feels, will be created only though an acute
awareness of the past. Saul echoes her thoughts explicitly: "It's usually so
painful though: looking back and into yourself; most people run from it . . .
But sometimes it's necessary to go back before you can go forward, really
forward. And that's not only true for people—individuals—but nations as
well . . ." Since Miss Marshall believes that without tradition one has no

real existence, she has all her major characters go back to their ancient heritage.

Time and again, Paule Marshall brings us to the question of human relationships. Beyond the barriers of race, all men are the same; they share the same fears, the same loneliness, and the same hopes. And they cannot live as islands; the bridges of communication have to be built. She repeatedly stresses the act of "using each other." In the complexity of human relationships we use each other in strange ways. Selina's affair with Clive is a way of getting even with her mother, while Clive needs to relieve his youthful aspirations through Selina. While Merle and Saul use each other to assuage their hurts and pains, Reena's boyfriend associates with her to annoy his father. But then Reena confesses with candor that she too has used him "to get at that white world which had not only denied me, but had turned my own against me." Despite these varied uses, the truth is that we need to share ourselves with others, barring which the life is a barren wasteland. However, sharing is by no means easy, for it means adding to one's sorrows.

*The Chosen Place* . . . also deals with the question of Western aid to the so-called underdeveloped countries. One cannot help wondering if the aid is meaningful and fruitful when an outsider tries to impose a new way of life to obliterate the centuries-old systems and values. The conflict between the old and the new assumes such proportions that the entire purpose is lost. Several attempts to modernize Bournehills have failed because the Americans have never tried to understand the place. Saul succeeds because he accepts the existing way of life and builds upon it.

Leela Kapai, "Dominant Themes and Technique in Paule Marshall's Fiction," *CLA Journal* 16, No. 1 (September 1972): 54–55

---

**PAULE MARSHALL**      In order to talk about what I believe to be some of the important early influences which shape my work, it will be necessary to take a giant step back to that stage in life when, without being conscious of it, I began the never-ending apprenticeship which is writing. It began in of all places the ground floor kitchen of a brownstone house in Brooklyn. Let me try to recreate the setting for you. Picture if you will a large old-fashioned kitchen with a second-hand refrigerator, the kind they used to have back then in the thirties with the motor on top, a coal stove that in its blackness, girth and the heat it threw off during the winter overwhelmed the gas range next to it, a sink whose pipes never ceased their rusty cough and a large table covered in flowered oilcloth set like an altar in the middle of the room.

It was at this table that the faithful, my mother and her women friends, would gather almost every afternoon upon returning from their jobs as domestics—or to use their term for the work they did "scrubbing Jew floor." Their work day had begun practically at dawn with the long train ride out to the white sections of Brooklyn. There, the ones who weren't lucky enough to have a steady job would stand on the street corners waiting in the cold— if it was winter—for the white, mainly Jewish housewives to come along and hire them for a half day's work cleaning their houses. The auction block was still very real for them.

Later, armed with the few dollars they had earned, my mother and her friends would make the long trip back to our part of town and there, in the sanctuary of our kitchen, talk endlessly, passionately. I didn't realize it then but those long afternoon rap sessions were highly functional, therapeutic; they were, you might even say, a kind of magic rite, a form of juju, for it was their way to exorcise the day's humiliations and restore them to themselves. ⟨. . .⟩

Moreover, all that free-wheeling talk together with the sometimes bawdy jokes and the laughter which often swept the kitchen was, at its deepest level, an affirmation of their own worth; it said that they could not be either demeaned or defeated by the daily trip out to Flatbush. It declared that they had retained and always would a strong sense of their special and unique Black identity.

I could understand little of this at the time. Those mysterious elements I heard resonating behind the words, which held me spellbound, came across mainly as a feeling which entered me it seemed not only through my ears but through the pores of my skin (I used to get goose pimples listening to them at times) to become part of my blood. It sings there to this day. I couldn't define it then, but I know now that contained in that feeling were those qualities which Black people possess no matter where you find them in the hemisphere—and which to my mind make of us one people.

Paule Marshall, "Shaping the World of My Art," New Letters 40, No. 1 (Autumn 1973): 97–98, 104

---

**BARBARA CHRISTIAN**     The interrelatedness of complex shapes and settings is so fused in Marshall that her books are verbal sculptures.

Form and space and humanity and culture cannot be separated. Her words chisel features, crevices, lines, into the grand, seemingly formless mass of history. Certainly marked in *Brown Girl, Brownstones*, this sculpted effect is the dominant formal chracteristic of *The Chosen Place, the Timeless People*. The land is the people, the people the land. Yet complexity and individuality of character are not sacrificed to largeness of theme. The intricacy of detail is maintained, even extended, in Marshall's panoramic novel. ⟨. . .⟩ Marshall's analysis is powerful because she so profoundly loves her characters, and she insists, throughout her work, that social themes are distorted if not fused with the complexity of individual human beings. ⟨. . .⟩

Paule Marshall's works, as psychopolitical images, elucidate the people who affect their culture and are affected in turn by their creation. Because of this thrust, her works remind us that all of us compose our own experiences in our minds and that our individual shapes are kinetically poised in a unified sculpture called the universe; that we all are continuity and process, shape and space, and that our sculpted creations are ourselves; that we change our world by changing our shapes, yet our world will change whether or not we want it to. Marshall's novels manifest history as a creative and moral process, for she graphically describes how we compose our own experiences in our minds as well as in the objective world; how we as individuals and whole cultures decide upon the moral nature of an act, a series of acts, a history. Above all, her work shows us that creative writing must be immersed in an act of honesty and love. The new child will come, when it has a mind to.

> Barbara Christian, "Sculpture and Space: The Interdependency of Character and Culture in the Novels of Paule Marshall," *Black Women Novelists: The Development of a Tradition 1892–1976* (Westport, CT: Greenwood Press, 1980), pp. 134–36

---

**DARRYL PINCKNEY**     In exploring the stages of black women's lives, Marshall insists that the woman with enough nerve can win even when the deck is stacked and the other players are hostile. Nerve, here, means making radical choices, and though the liberating destinies Marshall gives to her heroines are often unconvincing, the attraction of her work lies in a deep saturation in the consciousness of her characters and the ability to evoke the urban or tropical settings in which they toil. Dorothy Parker, in a review of the first novel, complained about the title. The years have not improved Marshall's ear for titles. They are sentimental and heavy with obvious meaning. They do not do justice to the discipline of the writing or to Marshall's engagement with questions of heritage, assimilation, and the black woman's identity.

Marshall's heroines tend to be stubborn, alienated, and ripe for some sort of conversion. The leap of faith is presented as a matter of making up one's mind to heed an inner voice, whatever the cost. Unfortunately, these assured, preachy women are not as interesting as the flawed souls who surround them and hold them down. ⟨. . .⟩

Virginia Woolf once observed that when women come to write novels, they probably find themselves wanting to alter established values, to make important what is insignificant to men and to make trivial what men think essential. Marshall shares this subversive inclination and sometimes it brings satisfying results. But Woolf also warned against a distorting element that can enter the fiction of those who are painfully aware of their "disability," and in Marshall's case the distorting element is not only a simplistic view of culture but also a simplistic idea of strength. The women in her novels are meant to seem courageous, but they have more of the manic certitude of religious fanatics. They have an almost narcissistic appreciation of their own states of mind but little is revealed about the complicated forces against which they claim to struggle. This limited picture of the world is what sets Marshall's women apart from those of Zora Neale Hurston, whose women are more tolerant, forgiving, and, one might say, truly experienced.

Perhaps this one-dimensional approach comes from current strains in black feminism. To counter the image of the black woman as victim, a different picture is deemed necessary, one that inadvertently makes such words as "nurturing," "positive," and "supportive" unbearable. One is constantly aware of a manipulation of reality at work in Marshall's fiction and this causes us to distrust it.

Darryl Pinckney, "Roots," *New York Review of Books*, 28 April 1983, pp. 26, 29–30

---

**SUSAN WILLIS**     Marshall demonstrates deep political understanding in *Brown Girl, Brownstones* by showing that the desire to own property may well have represented an initial contestation of bourgeois white domination, but because property ownership is implicit in capitalist society, the moment of opposition was immediately absorbed and integrated into the context of American capitalism. As long as white property owners could move out to the suburbs, it mattered little—nor did it represent a transformation of the system—that black people might be establishing parallel property systems in the cities. Marshall shows great sensitivity in demonstrating how the desire for property is lived as a passion, whose result is the repression of sexuality and the transformation of a loving, supportive couple relationship into one defined by deceit and treachery. Marshall's great talent as a writer is to show how broad historical developments are lived by families—and particularly by women in their roles as daughters and mothers. When we read *Brown Girl, Brownstones*, we cannot help but be amazed at the power of Silla's desire to "buy house," to be a full citizen like her neighbors, who, on their way up and out of poverty, ape middle-class modes of behavior. We cannot help but be struck by the horrible dissension the mother's project unleashes, which has its culmination in Silla's betrayal of her husband and Selina's denunciation of her mother as a "Hitler." And finally, we cannot help but be dumbfounded at Silla's brutal denial of self—her self-sacrifice, never allowing herself a moment's frivolity; her toil, taking on long hours and difficult jobs; and finally her repression of sexuality. Her refusal to have sex with her husband seems all the more self-negating when we see Silla, as Marshall portrays her during a wedding reception, dancing with delightful abandon and deep sensuality. Caught up in the all-consuming obsession to save every nickel and dime and to convert her husband's piece of land in Barbados into a down payment on a New York brownstone, Silla becomes a living embodiment of compulsive desires, some of which (like her frugality and possessiveness) she probably inherited with her peasant origins, but all of which dovetail with the demands of capitalism. The beauty of Marshall's portrayal is to make us ever aware of Silla's deeply human passions, which have been repressed or distorted in her relentless drive to ascend to the middle class.

Susan Willis, "Describing Arcs of Recovery: Paule Marshall's Relationship to Afro-American Culture," *Specifying: Black Women Writing the American Experience* (Madison: University of Wisconsin Press, 1987), pp. 74–75

---

**DARWIN T. TURNER**      In *Brown Girl, Brownstones* (1959), ⟨. . .⟩ Marshall tells the story of a Black family whose problems are not uniquely those of Black Americans. The mother, Serena Boyce, has come to America in search of the American Dream: through hard work, discipline, and frugal management, she and her family will acquire property, respectability, and a new home. Her immigrant husband, Deighton Boyce, however, wants only to earn enough money to be able to return to his homeland, where he can flaunt his affluence before his neighbors. Torn between the values of these two, their daughter Selina must also experience the problems of a young woman growing to physical, intellectual, psychological, and cultural maturity.

In her focus on Selina's growth, Marshall seems to anticipate *Bildungsromans* of Black women. That is, despite a few notable exceptions, such as Zora Neale Hurston in *Their Eyes Were Watching God* (1937), most Black women authors who wrote about Black women protagonists before 1950 concentrated on their adult lives. Even in *The Street* (1946), Ann Petry sketched only enough of Lutie Johnson's early life to enable a reader to learn something about her values, their source, and her reason for an early marriage. Four years after *Brown Girl, Brownstones*, Mary Elizabeth Vroman, in *Esther* (1963), revealed her protagonist's intellectual and emotional development from the age of thirteen into her adult life. In *God Bless the Child* (1964), Kristin Hunter portrayed Rosie Fleming from the age of seven until her death as a young woman. In the 1980s, when readers familiar with Black literature automatically think of such novels as Toni Morrison's *Sula* (1974) or Alice Walker's *The Color Purple* (1982), a story exploring the maturing of a Black woman does not seem unusual. In 1959, however, Marshall was among the earliest to trace such development.

Darwin T. Turner, "Introduction," *Soul Clap Hands and Sing* by Paule Marshall (Washington, DC: Howard University Press, 1988), pp. xxii–xxiii

---

**MISSY DEHN KUBITSCHEK**          In her depictions of female quests, Marshall follows Hurston in making storytelling central. Listening to stories motivates some questers; telling stories helps to heal others; above all, the sense of community involved in the participatory interchange of teller and audience strengthens the questers' identities. In *Brown Girl,* with its adolescent quester, older characters generally tell stories to younger ones; in *Chosen Place,* the middle-aged exchange stories. Selina must absorb the narratives of her parents and their generation, and Merle must draw out and contribute to the flow of personal stories in her mostly middle-aged circle.

Merle's search for her daughter, however, implies subsequent participation in the intergenerational pattern: questers do not choose one pattern or the other, but participate in each at different stages in their lives or in different roles during the same stage. *Praisesong* exalts the intergenerational narrative by making it Avatara's vocation. Both her process in claiming it and her conception of storytelling's purposes, however, diverge from those of Marshall's earlier novels and from a large portion of other African-American fiction. All three of Marshall's novels emphasize the integral relationship of storytelling and the female quest. Collaboratively constructing stories, both tribal and individual, furthers the development of both community and individual. The quester must find an empowering, participatory audience to help her articulate her own destiny within its larger destiny.

> Missy Dehn Kubitschek, "Paule Marshall's Witness to History," *Claiming the Heritage: African-American Women Novelists and History* (Jackson: University Press of Mississippi, 1991), pp. 70–71

**SUSAN FROMBERG SCHAEFFER**     Paule Marshall's *Daughters* is that rarity, a good *and* important book. It attempts to look at black experience in our hemisphere, to praise what progress has been made and to point to what yet needs to be done. In its willingness to take real stock, to find true answers to complex questions, it is a brave, intelligent and ambitious work.

Ms. Marshall examines the state of black life through Ursa Mackenzie, whose heritage—and perhaps nature—is dual. Her father, Primus Mackenzie, is a prominent official of a mythical Caribbean island, Triunion; he has been known since his youth as "the PM." Her mother is the American-born Estelle Harrison, who sends a very young Ursa back to the United States so that her child can learn "to talk the talk and walk the walk." Most of all, Estelle does not want Ursa to grow up to be a Triunion woman, one who waits hand and foot on her man and who has little independence of thought or deed. It is as if Estelle knows that her daughter will have a special role to play in determining the fate of black people in one or both of her countries. She is determined to make a difference. ⟨. . .⟩

*Daughters* seems to imply that the purpose of many unions should now be mutual struggle; struggle, if necessary, *against* each other but always toward an ideal. Black men, who entered the political and economic arenas earlier than black women, have greater temptations to contend with and are thus more likely to be seduced from their ideals. Through Primus and Estelle Mackenzie, Ms. Marshall shows us how the *women* can—and perhaps should—find themselves becoming men's consciences. ⟨. . .⟩

⟨. . .⟩ Women, Ms. Marshall shows us, spend more of their time than men with children, friends and family. They are less likely to be distracted from what was probably always their original goal: to be of use.

Yet even here, women are hampered by the inevitable facts of life: they love and are sexually attracted to their husbands and fathers, and, unless they can free themselves from the spells of men, they are of little use as consciences. And so, when Estelle decides to move against her husband, to keep him "on the straight and narrow," she cannot do it. It is at this point that Estelle calls upon her daughter to act when she cannot. ⟨. . .⟩

Many ideas dominate this wonderful novel, but perhaps the most important is that we have been on the wrong road, a "bypass road" that allows us to travel through life without seeing the urgent needs of others. You close *Daughters* feeling as if you have taken a dangerous trip that cannot leave you unchanged. Flawless in its sense of place and character, remarkable in its understanding of human nature, *Daughters* is a triumph in every way.

Susan Fromberg Schaeffer, "Cutting Herself Free," New York Times Book Review, 27 October 1991, pp. 3, 29

---

**CAROL ASCHER**     *Daughters*, Marshall's fourth novel, is her most ambitious, mature and sharply political. It begins as small as the personal distress of a black woman, Ursa Mackenzie, returning from an abortion to her Upper West Side studio apartment in New York City. Single, in her thirties, temporarily jobless, Ursa is too paralyzed to return the call on her answering machine from her dear friend Viney Davis. She can only wait uselessly in the darkening evening for a ring from Lowell Carruthers, who has no reason to extend their relationship beyond a biweekly dinner and a little "company through the night," since she never even told him she was pregnant. Nor can Ursa open the one letter that lies among her junk mail: it's from her father, Primus Mackenzie, a politician on the small Caribbean island of Triunion, and a man she has always loved dearly. ⟨. . .⟩

From this tiny, isolated New York apartment, *Daughters* moves slowly outward in ever-widening circles that come to encompass relations, friends, lovers and colleagues in both the Caribbean and greater New York. Finally, this fictional world extends backward half a century, more, back to slavery itself, at the same time as it moves a mere two months forward, to election week on Triunion. Through the issues confronting Ursa's father, *Daughters* makes clear the dependent nature of Triunion as it grows poorer and more crowded over the years. (An American warship, the *Woody Wilson*, stands in the harbor at every election, ensuring that no candidate with wild socialist ideas, such as Primus once had, will win.) At the same time, we see life as it is lived at the increasingly compromised center of political power. Like Marshall's other books, *Daughters* prompts one to reflect on the life choices given to an African-American woman or man in both the metropolis and the colonies. ⟨. . .⟩

*Daughters* is intimately observed, culturally rich, morally serious. Marshall loves her complex, imperfect characters, male and female; she loves the tragic, often comic, worlds they inhabit. It is this love that one feels drives her to write so seriously and fully, and that makes each new work feel like the return of an old friend.

> Carol Ascher, "Compromised Lives," *Women's Review of Books* 9, No. 2 (November 1991): 7

# ▨ *Bibliography*

*Brown Girl, Brownstones.* 1959.
*Soul Clap Hands and Sing.* 1961.
*The Chosen Place, the Timeless People.* 1969.
*Praisesong for the Widow.* 1983.
*Reena and Other Stories.* 1983.
*Daughters.* 1991.

❖ ❖ ❖

# Willard Motley
## *1909–1965*

WILLARD FRANCIS MOTLEY was born on July 14, 1909 (although 1912 is frequently given erroneously as his year of birth), in Englewood, an ethnically mixed suburb of Chicago. Motley began writing at a very early age: he had a short story published in the *Chicago Defender* in 1922, and he wrote a weekly children's column in that magazine from 1922 to 1924. After graduating from Englewood High School in 1929 Motley began traveling around the United States writing short stories and working at a variety of jobs: migrant laborer, ranch hand, cook, shipping clerk, photographer, radio scriptwriter, and newspaper editor. He submitted his stories to a number of magazines and newspapers between 1930 and 1935; all were rejected. Subsequent travels in the West provided more experience and material, including a month-long jail sentence in Wyoming for vagrancy.

Motley returned to Chicago in 1939 and took a slum apartment at Fourteenth and Union. Using material from his travels, he wrote nonfiction articles for a variety of magazines. In 1940 he worked for the Federal Writers' Project, meeting Richard Wright, Arna Bontemps, and other black writers who encouraged him. He visited prisons and juvenile reformatories and spent time in Chicago's Italian district, Little Sicily. All this activity supplied the background for his first novel, *Knock on Any Door*. This work, based upon a two-part article he had published in the *Ohio Motorist* for August 1938 and May 1939 concerning a Mexican-American boy who was imprisoned for stealing a bicycle, was begun in 1940 and completed in 1942; after being rejected by several publishers, it was finally published in 1947. This highly naturalistic novel deals with a boy from a poor Italian family living in the slums of Chicago who is brutalized in reform school and is finally executed for killing a police officer; it was a tremendous critical and popular success and was eventually made into a film starring Humphrey Bogart.

Motley's second novel, *We Fished All Night* (1951), about postwar political and social life in Chicago, was less well received. A year after its appearance

Motley purchased a house near Mexico City and lived there the rest of his life. He never married, but he adopted a Mexican boy, Sergio Lopez.

*Let No Man Write My Epitaph* (1958), Motley's third novel, is a partial sequel to *Knock on Any Door*. It deals more explicitly with racial matters than either of his two previous novels. Although it was filmed in 1960, critical reception to it was unenthusiastic. Motley's last novel, *Let Noon Be Fair*, was published a year after his death in Mexico from intestinal gangrene on March 4, 1965. It deals with American exploitation of Mexico, the subject of Motley's unpublished nonfiction volume, *My House Is Your House*. An abridged edition of the diaries kept by Motley between 1926 and 1943 was published in 1979.

Although some black critics during his lifetime criticized Motley's novels for failing to treat racial matters directly, many later critics have praised his work for its grim realism, its sensitive character portrayal, and its depiction of a "raceless" society.

# ▨ *Critical Extracts*

**WILLARD MOTLEY**      Another year and a new series of diaries. A new series in that the past year has brought so many new influences, ideas, perspectives into my life that I have, in the full sense, grown up. Most important is my jump from the subjective to the objective both in thought and in my writing. The past year was a full one. Most prominent was the full evolvement of my novel, "Leave Without Illusions" ⟨working title for *Knock on Any Door*⟩, three chapters of which I have completed and the entire story of which is completely worked out to the last sentence. Have about 200 typed pages of scenes, dialogue and framework in a folder. Everything in the last year went into the story in one way or another. Hull House, meeting and becoming friends with Sandy ⟨novelist Alexander Saxton⟩, gaining Mike's friendship, following him home to see and study his parents, his home life, Halstead Street, West Madison Street, talks with Peter and Beatrice, intimate friendship with Matt, Joe, Alex, Tony, Concho, Andy, Johnny, opening the door to everyone, letting them in, listening to them talk—all this has brought knowledge and information to me. Tramps down West Madison, Halstead Street, Peoria, Newberry, Maxwell were wonderful.

Just walking and looking. Some of these walks were with Sandy. Impressions came in from everywhere. The neighborhood is a storehouse for a writer.

This one thing I learned last year, probably the most important thing that any writer who wants to get to the top must discover—

Some authors write at a great distance from their subjects, some very close to their subject. I want to write as part of my subject.

> Willard Motley, Diary entry (1 January 1941), *The Diaries of Willard Motley*, ed. Jerome Klinkowitz (Ames: Iowa State University Press, 1979), p. 165

---

**THOMAS D. JARRETT**     Characters that live and a plot that is credible make a good novel. One must believe in the characters and must find in them semblances or recordings of his own observations and experiences. In *Knock on Any Door*, Nick Romano, whose life is graphically drawn from the time that he is an altar boy at St. Augustine's to the moment that he pays the supreme penalty for a brutal murder, is real; we believe in him. Yet, if the reader is to grasp the full import of Motley's social preachment, he must have that preachment or message artistically presented to him by analogy and artful pictorialization rather than by marked sermonizing. This Motley does effectively. ⟨. . .⟩

It is true that such naturalists as Theodore Dreiser, James T. Farrell, and Richard Wright have, among other writers, compared man in society to a "trapped," helpless animal, who, as Dorothy Canfield Fisher says of characters like Bigger Thomas of *Native Son*, in their behavior patterns give "evidence of the same bewildered senseless tangle of abnormal nerve-reactions studied in animals by psychologists in laboratory experiments"; yet, in *An American Tragedy*, *Studs Lonigan* and *Native Son* there is not a utilization of a progressive and connected series of images. An image is used for momentary clarification of an idea or scene and is dropped. The technique employed by these authors does not evoke such a method, or, to put it another way, they have not chosen to set forth or bolster their preachments through the medium of sustained employment of imagery. Such is the novelist's prerogative. He may enhance or depreciate the value of his work by the technique employed. Undoubtedly, in *Knock on Any Door* it is Motley's employment of meaningful and colorful imagery more than any other single element in relation to character portrayal that vivifies his naturalistic social philosophy and expresses his piercing indictment of a society that breeds criminals and then butchers them. Through these well-chosen symbols the author's deterministic doctrine, finally expressed in the words of Nick's lawyer, is made crystal clear.

> ... Anyone can reason from cause to effect and know that the crimes of children are really the crimes of the State and Society, which by neglect and active participation have made the individual what he is .... Nick Romano awaits your decision. ... His life is but a little thing. ... His life is in your hands. If you choose you can snuff out his life.

Society chose to "snuff out" Nick's life, just as a sadistic schoolmate had, in the earlier part of the novel, stripped a fly of its wings, allowed it to crawl helplessly about, and finally dropped it into an inkwell. Nick could not free himself; yet, within the lonely confines of his death cell, he chose to free a little fly, ensnared in a spider web.

> Thomas D. Jarrett, "Sociology and Imagery in a Great American Novel," *English Journal* 38, No. 9 (November 1949): 518, 520

---

**CARL MILTON HUGHES**     In its own terms, *Knock on Any Door* posits the sociological case study of Nick Romano. In developing his thesis that environment conditions a sensitive boy negatively, Motley selects incidents where social custom is broken, the law flouted, and a man murdered in order to prove his case. The inherent elements in such an environment that could change a very sensitive boy, whose ambition was to become a priest, into a hardened criminal are slums, poverty, and ignorance. In another sense police brutality, parental neglect, and failure of the church must be brought into the picture, for they are guilty and responsible for Nick's tragic end, too.

Nick's development into a criminal who proudly faces the electric chair forms the first half of the methodical reporting of Motley in his *Knock on Any Door*. The picture in contrast from the sensitive altar boy, who was almost too handsome, to the conscienceless murderer presents one of the more effective and emotionally charged portrayals in modern American writing. ⟨. . .⟩

Motley is not a moralizer as such, but the social commentary in his novel, *Knock on Any Door*, strikes with unmistakable force. He follows the principles of the school of naturalism very closely. This set of circumstances without God and without successful educative forces makes of Nick a pawn in the hands of malevolent society. Nick makes the decision through the exercise of his own volition after he has been warped by society's agencies which are theoretically designed to mold character and to develop upright citizens. In this act Nick is determined in his course of development by the street. This means that in the end he does a fair amount of damage to himself and others. This gives to the naturalistic writer a case which not only has sociological content and implications for society but proves Motley's thesis that unwholesome environment corrupts youths and makes criminals of them. Motley's approach to the problem of living is very stark and realistic, and many who are dispossessed lose in the struggle for a decent and happy life. Indeed, Nick Romano is an example.

Society's institutions, when they are unsuccessful, produce cockiness in a person like Nick. This cockiness is characterized by his statement, "Live fast, die young, make a good-looking corpse." Such a statement indicates the extent of society's warping influence. Nick means that he is conscious of the reform school, and of his unpleasant home life, and the brutality of the police and his own fate. In another mood this is Nick enamored of free sex and easy money. He rejects conscience because he is in a state of mental confusion. He knows only the sordid side of life and can not ascertain his proper course. Society betrayed him by not offering him conditions which would permit him to develop into the priest which was the embodiment of good and his childish ambition. Nature is on the side of this criminal, for Nick is handsome and charming. This characterization shows the author's concern for the problem. It is out of compassion for those who inhabit the underworld, and who are doomed to untimely destruction, that he wants this condition improved, the corrupting influences eradicated. With his tremendous energy, Motley turns upon society and registers his disgust for such an environment.

Carl Milton Hughes, The Negro Novelist: A Discussion of the Writings of American Negro Novelists 1940–1950 (New York: Citadel Press, 1953), pp. 179–80, 184–85

---

**WALTER B. RIDEOUT**          In *Knock on Any Door*, Motley's concern for the hero as victim, though intense, is kept under artistic control; in his second and most recent novel *We Fished All Night* (1951), the control has slipped, or rather his material lies almost beyond his control. Here what he attempts is to tell, not the story of one main victim, but that of three. Furthermore, where Nick's fate illustrates a unified, if limited, philosophic conception, the fates of Aaron Levin, Don Lockwood, and Jim Norris are intended to encompass all the myriad frustrations, dislocations, alienations, and defeats which Motley sees young Americans subjected to in a particular complex moment in history, the aftermath of World War II. Aaron Levin, alienated from his fellow men by his sense of Jewishness, achieves the complete self-separation of mental derangement and suicide. Chet Kosinski, attempting to erase the effects of his squalid home environment, constructs an image of himself as "Don Lockwood," becomes the "liberal" cat's-paw of a political boss, builds a boss-machine of his own, marries a wealthy girl, and learns to live with his corruption. If Don's career is reminiscent of Dan Minturn's, Jim Norris's recalls in part that of the labor organizer in the proletarian strike novel, with one important difference. Jim too has been so emotionally warped by a war experience that he is incapable of adequate sex relations with his wife and must fight an almost uncontrollable perverse desire for young girls. Here the working-class protagonist has become almost as twisted by the horrors of total war as the capitalist Emerson Bradley has become through his power over the lives of others; yet Jim finds himself at last in the strike against the Bradley plant, only to meet the traditional death at the hands of the police in a strike riot.

Politically Motley's novel is orientated toward the Progressive Party. (By working for this cause in the 1948 elections, one of Don's rejected girl friends, the woman who knows him best, finds personal integration.) Such an orientation no doubt helped to offset his caustic portrait of a Communist novelist who writes "novels approved by the party," whose second novel is admittedly damaged by doctrinaire Marxism, and who himself states that he robs his characters of humanity by turning them into symbols. At any rate a left-wing reviewer, writing of *We Fished All Night* early in 1953, praised the book highly, but found his chief objection in the characterization of Jim. A "conscious idealist" like Norris, he argues, would have been more aware of war's brutalities and their tendency to produce psychic damage; hence, he would have been able to cope with his traumatic experience *before* it produced such devastating, if impermanent, results. Whether he knew it or not, this reviewer was demanding from Motley an idealized picture of the Communist hero, who became the most popular single subject for radical novelists from 1940 onward as though to compensate for the almost complete failure of the proletarian novel of the thirties to treat such a figure fully. Here also may be operating for the first time in the American radical novel an influence from Soviet fiction, which had been concerned throughout the thirties, and indeed still is, with the portrayal of "the new soviet man"; but at least one sharp difference divides the American heroes from the Russian: unlike the latter, the former still dwell in a prerevolutionary society and must fight a preëminently hostile environment, rather than respond to a preëminently friendly one.

Walter B. Rideout, *The Radical Novel in the United States 1900–1954* (Cambridge, MA: Harvard University Press, 1956), pp. 263–64

**CHESTER E. EISINGER**     Willard Motley's *Knock on Any Door* (1947), in which the characters are white, incidentally, voices its protest in all the stereotypes of naturalism. With plodding doggedness, Motley documents the overpowering influence of a slum environment on his hero who ends, predictably and at long last, in the electric chair. The odor of sensationalism is faintly in the air as Motley dredges up the various amusements of the lumpen proletariat when they while away the hours of their vicious idleness. Motley has discovered that since men are the victims of a bad society, we ought to have a good society. It is not fair to say that this kind of novel reveals the bankruptcy of naturalism, but since Motley invents no new things and casts no new light, one must conclude that naturalism is in serious trouble.

Chester E. Eisinger, *Fiction of the Forties* (Chicago: University of Chicago Press, 1963), p. 70

**CLARENCE MAJOR**     I remember the nervous pitch of Willard Motley's thin, soft voice; the almost effeminate way his mouth formed words, which reminded me also of Truman Capote's mouth forming sounds. Norman Ross was interviewing Motley once on his VIP show, and the novelist couldn't seem to get his voice above a whisper. Ross asked, "Why do you write about people around West Madison Street rather than about Negroes?" (i.e., as other Negro writers do). Motley said softly, "I find the plight of the people on West Madison *more* urgent." I almost fell off my chair. There he was, sitting there in his white silky-looking suit, like a butterscotch-colored South American tobacco-inspector, saying some shit like *that!* I turned to Grayson, who was also watching it, and I couldn't see his face, only the interior of his mouth—he was laughing so hard. Even my wife, in the kitchen making coffee, fell out.

> Clarence Major, "Willard Motley: Vague Ghost After the Father" (1969), *The Dark and Feeling: Black American Writers and Their Work* (New York: Third Press, 1974), p. 96

**NOEL SCHRAUFNAGEL**     The Wright school of protest is primarily limited to the depiction of racial exploitation. One popular novel by a black American during the decade, though, was Willard Motley's *Knock on Any Door* (1947). A protest novel in the tradition of Wright, it has one major difference. The characters, with a few minor exceptions, are white. The pattern of the protest novel has been changed little, however, and Motley has even been accused of stealing the plot from *Native Son*.

While the story of the depravity of the Italian youth is analogous to the plight of Bigger Thomas, *Knock on Any Door* is different in the sense that Romano is not surrounded by the aura of inferiority associated with the Negro. He is not branded by his color as a person to be despised and exploited. There are no myths that attest to his inherent worthlessness that can match those applied to a black boy. Romano's experiences tend to alienate him from respectable society, but much of his trouble is the result of his own ignorance and pride. Women love him and he has influential friends, but Nick rejects them all rather than lose his reputation for toughness. He wills his own death as a final act of defiance.

The rebellion of Nick Romano, then, is not the rebellion of Bigger Thomas: the Italian's battle is only in part with a hostile society. In essence, he rebels from everyone—from those who have helped him as well as those who have hurt him. His rebellion is in his choice of a life of crime and in his confession to the charge of murder. This is his way of asserting himself, but it is a negative assertion made by a youth to whom life is no longer desirable. The killing of the policeman is an act of destruction rather than of creation, and the confession to the act fulfills the unconscious aspirations for his own death. Unlike Bigger Thomas, who is just discovering himself and the meaning of his life at the time of his execution, Romano has known for too long what he is, and the truth sickens him. While Bigger develops into a metaphysical rebel, Nick lives as a weak facsimile of one until the futility of it becomes too much.

Noel Schraufnagel, *From Apology to Protest: The Black American Novel* (Deland, FL: Everett/Edwards, 1973), pp. 44–46

---

**JAMES R. GILES and KAREN MAGEE MYERS**      It is commonly agreed that Willard Motley's second novel, *We Fished All Night* (1951), is a failure. Despite its obvious flaws, however, the novel is still worthy of study for several related reasons. Most importantly, *We Fished All Night* is a striking example of one way in which the theory of literary naturalism can be misapplied. Motley's personal letters, a body of which are currently housed at Northern Illinois University, confirm that the novelist's flaws are due to authorial confusion regarding execution of thematic design, rather than to the design itself. The novel's intention of utilizing World War II as an unifying symbol is made immediately clear by its impressionistic opening sketch of a maimed returning soldier. However, the subsequent application of this introductory symbol is not always so apparent. Motley's letters indicate that the unnamed soldier's physical wounds are to represent the spiritual maiming of his main characters, and of the post-war world. In a letter to a friend, he outlines this concept: the war is a catalyst which activated the latent psychological wounds of his three main male characters, Don Lockwood, Aaron Levin, and Jim Norris. All the childhood guilts and fears (especially concerning sex) of the three men are unleashed by the brutality of experience in combat, effecting a subconscious need to return to a protected world of childish innocence. 〈. . .〉

Motley's failure with Jim Norris offers an unique insight into the limitations of the novel and the novelist. For most of *We Fished All Night* Norris is the only character who is sympathetic as well as believable. Motley's letters reveal an admiration for Hemingway, and Jim Norris is an illustration of the influence. In fact, Norris projects a masculinity that is all the more attractive because it is *not* rooted in "big-game-hunter toughness." Of all Hemingway characters, he is perhaps most reminiscent of Robert Jordan. One Motley letter describes Norris as "idealistic" and a "moral man," whose idealism is intensified by feelings of childhood guilt and by the horrors of warfare. Like Aaron, he throws himself into "good causes." Jim Norris returns from World War II and becomes a fiery labor agitator in the struggle against fascism at home; Robert Jordan goes to Spain to defeat European fascism.

Motley's problems with the Norris characterization emerge in the latter part of the novel. From the first, Motley had intended Norris to be a victim of "sexual aberration"—a barely-controlled need for increasingly younger girls leading inexorably to child-molestation. The initial "explanation" for this sickness was to have been Norris' war-time experience with a French prostitute, whom he sleeps with and then discovers to be only fourteen years old. If Motley had allowed this incident to suffice, Jim's "aberration" would have served well as a symbol of the novel's central theme—the war as destroyer of a world still immature, a holocaust so complete that even the idealists seduce children. ⟨. . .⟩

In the novel's last section, the Norris characterization is flawed in several ways. Part of the problem is Motley's attempt to dramatize Jim's central dualism: Norris struggles to control his urge to molest a child, while functioning heroically in a strike. While Motley has been unjustly accused of reducing Freudianism to a "Hollywood level" in his best work, the climactic scene in the Norris characterization could have come from hundreds of American "B films" of the thirties and forties. After stalking a little girl for several blocks, Jim controls himself at the last moment and leaves her unmolested. He then returns to the strike.

James R. Giles and Karen Magee Myers, "Naturalism as Principle and Trap: The Theory and Execution in Willard Motley's *We Fished All Night*," *Studies in Black Literature* 7, No. 1 (Winter 1976): 19, 21

---

**N. JILL WEYANT**     Often dismissed from serious critical consideration because of its crude style and sensational subject matter, Willard Motley's third novel, *Let No Man Write My Epitaph* (1957), should perhaps be reexamined before it is rejected altogether. There are several practical reasons why *Epitaph* is the weakest of Motley's four published novels. The fact that it is a sequel to Motley's astoundingly successful *Knock on Any Door* (1947) perhaps condemned *Epitaph* to the region of the second rate from the outset (are sequels ever as good as their originals?). Furthermore, the decision to write a sequel to *Knock* was dictated in large part by Motley's desperate financial situation in 1952 when *Epitaph* was begun. Frankly, *Epitaph* was written to make money, and Motley's poverty may help account for *Epitaph*'s tone, which is noticeably more bitter than in the other novels, the focus on then-explosive social problems like the heroin trade and misce-genation, and the undisguised plagiarism from *Knock*, the novel that brought wealth to its publisher but not to its author. And, with his melodramatic approach and stereotyped characters, including the arch-villain Frank Ram-poni, Motley seems to be appealing to society's least common denominator and to be lowering the intellectual level of the novel, possibly hoping that this might sell the book.

However, there are more complex psychological reasons why *Epitaph* is one of the most confused and confusing novels ever written. If carefully examined in light of Motley's personal development as revealed in his manuscripts and private papers, *Epitaph* reflects a transitional stage in Mot-ley's thinking from racial naïveté to an acute awareness of racism, or, to use more familiar terms, from innocence to experience. In many ways, Motley seems to be a case of delayed development, going through this initiation much later in his life than most other post-Renaissance Black writers (aged 40 when he began this novel, Motley was no adolescent when he underwent racial maturation) and much, much later than might be expected in light of the direction pointed early in the '40s by the ascendence of Richard Wright. The confusion in *Epitaph* might reflect Motley's state of mind at this time, but more important in a critical sense, *Epitaph* manifests Black pride and Black consciousness in Motley *for the first time* in print and shows him pivoting from writing novels of white life with only an occasional Black character (*Knock*; *We Fished All Night*, 1951) to a more fully developed examination of racial exploitation (culminating in the Mexican novel *Let Noon Be Fair*, 1966). In *Epitaph* Motley alternates between white charac-ters—Nick Romano's son Nick, Jr., and brother Louie—and Black charac-ters. The long sections on the suffering of the Black community represent Motley's delayed acceptance of his own racial identity as well as his arrival at a truer understanding of racial relations in racist America. This under-standing is absolutely crucial to Motley's literary development, for without it, he would have been doomed to remain a second-rate novelist lacking depth, to continue to move in circles groping to recapture the almost accidental success of his admittedly powerful but thematically and structur-ally simplistic first novel *Knock*. *We Fished All Night* and *Epitaph* were literary regressions for Motley, but his last novel *Noon*, written after the transition I see in *Epitaph*, seems to be a step forward in structure and theme that might have been improved on in other novels, had he lived to write on.

N. Jill Weyant, "Willard Motley's Pivotal Novel: *Let No Man Write My Epitaph*," *Black American Literature Forum* 11, No. 2 (Summer 1977): 56

**ROBERT E. FLEMING**     It was an unfortunate accident that Motley's favored subject matter and his most effective style belonged to an
earlier age. Had he been born thirty or even ten years earlier, he would not
have seemed such an anachronism. As his career developed, however, many
of his contemporaries benefited from the various experiments of James Joyce,
William Faulkner, John Dos Passos, and Ernest Hemingway to produce
works that eclipsed the Naturalistic novels of the preceding generation. The
type of novel that collected a huge body of evidence, that multiplied similar
incidents and amassed detail in order to create its effect, was abandoned
by most serious novelists of Motley's generation in favor of works that
utilized more impressionistic and selective techniques. The characteristic
attitudes and style of Naturalism were taken over by the hack writers who
exaggerated and prostituted the explicit violence and the sex that had been
a necessary part of novels by authors such as Frank Norris and Theodore
Dreiser. Of Motley's contemporaries, perhaps only James T. Farrell and John
O'Hara, whose own critical reputation is hardly secure, successfully labored
on as practicing Naturalists of the old school. For a young writer beginning
his career in the 1940s, to write Naturalistic novels was to relegate oneself
to second class status among American novelists.

But the best of Motley's novels, *Knock on Any Door*, belongs as firmly
in the older tradition as do Crane's *Maggie: A Girl of the Streets*, Norris's
*McTeague*, Dreiser's *An American Tragedy*, Farrell's *Studs Lonigan*, or
Wright's *Native Son*. Motley was not enough of an intellectual to devise a
new voice for himself, nor was he unprincipled and imitative enough to
ape the techniques developed by others. Finally, he lacked the stubborn
tenacity that has enabled James T. Farrell to transcend similar limitations
and produce a body of fiction that will probably earn him a reputation as
a writer of minor American classics. Instead, after the publication of his
first novel, Motley experimented uneasily with alien techniques that never
quite suited his material and expressed himself in a way that was never
again as heartfelt as the voice he had found in *Knock on Any Door*.

Robert E. Fleming, *Willard Motley* (Boston: Twayne, 1978), pp. 143–44

---

**JEROME KLINKOWITZ**     In 1926, at age sixteen, Motley began
a set of diaries that were to be faithfully continued until 1942, the year he
completed his first and best-selling novel, *Knock on Any Door*. "Awful

lonesome; need a chum," wrote Motley on his diary's first page, and he proceeded for seventeen years to create and sustain a personal, sometimes imaginary world. Facts are duly recorded; team sports, his adolescent newspaper work, school friendships, transcontinental trips, and an interminable series of projects. All, he is led to admit, are his own substitute for simple, natural companionship, and so as the years and the volumes of his diary draw on he becomes the self-conscious artist, weaving impossible ambitions (great romantic loves, a spectacular college career) not as a record of fact but as his life might be, as it "ought" to be. Always counterposed are the events—depression economics, growing racial complications to love— which make of Motley a hard-nosed realist at the same time he strikes his lofty ideals.

Willard Motley graduated from Englewood High School in Chicago on January 31, 1929, and after a year and a half of fruitless attempts to find a steady job, he set about collecting experiences and adventures for his stories. In June and July of 1930 he bicycled to New York, with no money and only the generosity of strangers, themselves experiencing the first summer of the Great Depression, to see him through. In the fall of 1933 he made an abortive, almost explicitly fantastical attempt to attend the University of Wisconsin as a spontaneous football hero. Through high school Motley had submitted scores of stories to *Boy's Life* and similar periodicals, although very few were ever accepted and published. Nevertheless he lived his life as material for fiction, and when he dreamed of himself as a great writer it was not simply a goal, but as a way of creating the very substance he wished to write about. His experiences in New York, in Madison, and ultimately on a nine-month hobo trip (repeated a year later) to California, Colorado, and the Pacific Northwest yielded much material for stories, often transcribed directly from his diaries.

Jerome Klinkowitz, "Introduction," *The Diaries of Willard Motley*, ed. Jerome Klinkowitz (Ames: Iowa State University Press, 1979), p. xvii

---

**ADAM MEYER**     Willard Motley was Black, but he didn't write very much about Black people. His motto was "people are just people," and so he felt himself justified in creating characters from backgrounds other than his own. Because he was thus unwilling to do what a Black writer is supposed to do, that is to show "Black" life, Motley has frequently been grouped with the other members of what some critics have termed the "raceless novel" movement of the late 1940s. This appellation, however, is very misleading. It may be true that, while Blacks are present in all of Motley's novels, the question of race was not a central theme in any of them, yet a critic who writes that "most of Motley's characters were white" ⟨Clarence Major⟩ is in error. What such a critic fails to take into account, as do the majority of Motley's readers, is that Motley "relates [racial] prejudice to ethnic prejudice"; he feels, for example, that "to scorn a man because he comes from south of the Mexican border is just as ridiculous as to 'jim-crow' him because he is black," a multi-ethnic concern which is "a fact not stressed by many racial spokesmen" ⟨Robert E. Fleming⟩. Almost all of Motley's major characters, unlike the white characters in James Baldwin's *Giovanni's Room* for example, or such relatively minor white characters as Grant Holloway in *Knock on Any Door*, come from a distinct ethnic background. Motley is clearly "substitut[ing] other minority groups for blacks to illustrate the effects of prejudice and oppression" ⟨Noel Schraufnagel⟩. ⟨. . .⟩

To call Motley a "raceless" writer, then, and to imply that he therefore has nothing to tell us about the racial and ethnic experiences in America, is to dismiss him far too casually. The reason Motley's Blackness poses a problem to us as readers and critics is that he confounds our expectations of ethnic literatures. Rather than not reading Motley, however, we need to examine and reassess the assumptions about ethnic literatures that have created these expectations.

Adam Meyer, "The Need for Cross-Ethnic Studies: A Manifesto (with Antipasto)," *MELUS* 16, No. 4 (Winter 1989–90): 20–21

# ▣ *Bibliography*

*Knock on Any Door*. 1947.
*We Fished All Night*. 1951.
*Let No Man Write My Epitaph*. 1958.
*Let Noon Be Fair*. 1966.
*Diaries*. Ed. Jerome Klinkowitz. 1979.

# Ann Petry
## *b. 1912*

ANN PETRY was born Ann Lane on October 12, 1912, in Old Saybrook, Connecticut. Her father was a pharmacist who operated his own drugstore, so that the Lanes were generally accepted by the white population of Old Saybrook in spite of the fact that they were only one of two black families in the small town. Several other members of Ann's family were also pharmacists. Ann began writing stories and poems while at Old Saybrook High School, from which she graduated in 1929; she then decided to pursue the family career by attending the College of Pharmacy of the University of Connecticut. She received a Ph.G. degree in 1931 and worked for seven years at her family's pharmacies in Old Saybrook and Lyme.

In 1938 Ann married the mystery writer George D. Petry; they have one daughter. Petry moved to Harlem, writing advertising copy for the *Amsterdam News* from 1938 to 1941 and being a reporter for the *People's Voice* from 1941 to 1946 while writing short stories in her spare time. Her first published story was "Marie of the Cabin Club," appearing in the *Afro-American* for August 19, 1939, under the pseudonym Arnold Petri. In 1943 she enrolled in a writing course at Columbia University; shortly thereafter, she was publishing stories in the *Crisis, Opportunity, Phylon,* and other journals. Petry's nonliterary life was also busy, as she formed a political group, Negro Women, Inc., lent assistance to a Harlem elementary school, and acted in an American Negro Theater production.

One of Petry's stories, "On Saturday the Siren Sounds at Noon," came to the attention of Houghton Mifflin, which invited her to apply for one of its literary fellowships. The synopsis and first five chapters of what would become Petry's first novel, *The Street,* won her the Houghton Mifflin Literary Fellowship. The novel was published in 1946 and received highly favorable reviews as a sensitive portrayal of a black woman's life in Harlem. The next year she published *Country Place,* a novel about small-town life in Connecticut; although all the major characters are white, Petry draws heavily upon her early life in Old Saybrook for many social and topographical details. In 1953 her third novel, *The Narrows*, appeared. Dealing with an interracial affair between a black man and a white woman in Connecticut, it is perhaps Petry's most complex and ambitious novel.

In the late 1940s Petry began to turn her attention to children's works, and she has produced *The Drugstore Cat* (1949), *Harriet Tubman: Conductor of the Underground Railroad* (1955), *Tituba of Salem Village* (1964), and *Legends of the Saints* (1970). Both her earlier and her later stories for adults were collected in *Miss Muriel and Other Stories* (1971).

Ann Petry left Harlem and returned to Old Saybrook in 1948, where she continues to reside with her husband.

# ▧ *Critical Extracts*

**JAMES W. IVY**      In person Mrs. Petry is of medium height, pleasant manners and intercourse, and possessed of a sense of companionable good humor. She has a creamy-brown complexion; alert, smiling eyes; and a soft cultivated voice. We entered at once into the intimacy of talk and the first thing I wanted to know was how she had come to write her first published story ("On Saturday the Siren Sounds at Noon").

"Did you have any particular message in that story? What were you trying to show?"

"Nothing in particular. I wrote it simply as a story. But it came to be written in this way. One Saturday I was standing on the 125th Street platform of the IRT subway when a siren suddenly went off. The screaming blast seemed to vibrate inside people. For the siren seemed to be just above the station. I immediately noticed the reactions of the people on the platform. They were interesting, especially the frantic knitting of a woman seated on a nearby bench.

"I began wondering," continued Mrs. Petry, "how this unearthly howl would affect a criminal, a man hunted by the police. That was the first incident. The second was a tragedy I covered for my paper. There was a fire in Harlem in which two children had been burnt to death. Their parents were at work and the children were alone. I imagined their reactions when they returned home that night. I knew also that many Harlem parents, like

Lilly Belle in the story, often left their children home alone while at work. Imaginatively combined the two incidents gave me my story." ⟨. . .⟩

I then asked her about her recently published novel, *The Street*.

"In *The Street* my aim is to show how simply and easily the environment can change the course of a person's life. For this purpose I have made Lindy Johnson an intelligent, ambitious, attractive woman with a fair degree of education. She lives in the squalor of 116th Street, but she retains her self-respect and fights to bring up her little son decently.

"I try to show why the Negro has a high crime rate, a high death rate, and little or no chance of keeping his family unit intact in large northern cities. There are no statistics in the book through they are present in the background, not as columns of figures but in terms of what life is like for people who live in over-crowded tenements.

"I tried to write a story that moves swiftly so that it would hold the attention of people who might ordinarily shy away from a so-called problem novel. And I hope that I have created characters who are real, believable, alive. For I am of the opinion that most Americans regard Negroes as types—not quite human—who fit into a special category and I wanted to show them as people with the same capacity for love and hate, for tears and laughter, and the same instinct for survival possessed by all men."

James W. Ivy, "Ann Petry Talks about First Novel," *Crisis* 53, No. 1 (January 1946): 48–49

---

**ARNA BONTEMPS**   The young woman's fight against the corrupting influences of this crowded little world, her effort to safeguard her son and to keep herself unsoiled, is the challenging theme Miss Petry has chosen for her novel ⟨*The Street*⟩. She could scarcely have found a more important human problem in our urban life today. She has treated it with complete seriousness in a story that will bear a lot of thoughtful reading.

As a novelist Miss Petry is an unblushing realist. Her recreation of the street has left out none of its essential character. It is a part of her achievement, however, that the carnal life of the slum never seems to be hauled in for its own sake. Even the earthy language, like something overheard on a truck or in a doorway, fails to draw attention to itself; in every case it seems to blend into the situation. It will not be for such details that *The Street* will be read and discussed.

Arna Bontemps, "Tough, Carnal Harlem," *New York Herald Tribune Weekly Book Review*, 10 February 1946, p. 4

**WRIGHT MORRIS**     Her first novel, *The Street*, published several years ago, attracted well-deserved praise—and, though it dealt with the familiar elements of the Negro-problem novel, it seemed to point the way to a brilliant creative future. But *The Narrows* reads like the first draft of an ambitious conception that has not been labored into imaginative life. It indicates what the author might have done but did not do. The forces that have lowered the craft of fiction have made it more difficult, not less, to write the book that will cry havoc and be heard. Miss Petry can do it, but it will take more brooding labor—and less space.

Wright Morris, "The Complexity of Evil," *New York Times Book Review*, 16 August 1953, p. 4

**MARY ROSS**     Ann Petry is a native New Englander with generations of New Englanders behind her. She started her career in chemistry. But the New England life of which she writes, in a small Connecticut city two hours' drive from New York, could be equally alien to the founding fathers and the suave commuters and summer people who now bowl along its highways. The "chemistry" of this remarkable novel ⟨*The Narrows*⟩ is something not learned in science books. ⟨. . .⟩

Mrs. Petry, using a theme that might have been merely sensational, builds a novel that has depth and dignity. There is power and insight and reach of imagination in her writing. Most white readers will find themselves in a world that has been closed to them, a world with its own beauty and strength and honor and humor, as well as its pathos and frustration. *The Narrows* is not an apologia for the Negro nor anything so simple as an indictment of the white race. It has no concern with posing or solving a "problem." It is a novel that stands on its own feet and it is an unusual and stirring experience. I have not read Ann Petry's earlier novel, *The*

*Street*, but I shall do so as soon as I can, and I shall look forward to her future work eagerly.

Mary Ross, "Depth and Dignity, Pathos and Humor," *New York Herald Tribune Book Review*, 16 August 1953, p. 3

---

**ANN PETRY**      In recent years, many novels of social criticism have dealt with race relations in this country. It is a theme which offers the novelist a wide and fertile field; it is the very stuff of fiction, sometimes comic, more often tragic, always ironic, endlessly dramatic. The setting and the characters vary in these books but the basic story line is derived from *Uncle Tom's Cabin*; discrimination and/or segregation (substitute slavery for the one or the other) are evils which lead to death—actual death or potential death. The characters either conform to the local taboos and mores and live, miserably; or refuse to conform and die.

This pattern of violence is characteristic of the type for a very good reason. The arguments used to justify slavery still influence American attitudes toward the Negro. If I use the words intermarriage, mixed marriage, miscegenation, there are few Americans who would not react to those words emotionally. Part of that emotion can be traced directly to the days of slavery. And if emotion is aroused merely by the use of certain words, and the emotion is violent, apoplectic, then it seems fairly logical that novels which deal with race relations should reflect some of this violence.

As I said, my first novel was a novel of social criticism. Having written it, I discovered that I was supposed to know the answer to many of the questions that are asked about such novels. What good do they do is a favorite. I think they do a lot of good. Social reforms have often received their original impetus from novels which aroused the emotions of a large number of readers. *Earth and High Heaven*, *Focus*, and *Gentleman's Agreement* undoubtedly made many a person examine the logic of his own special brand of anti-Semitism. The novels that deal with race relations have influenced the passage of the civil rights bills which have become law in many states.

Ann Petry, "The Novel as Social Criticism," *The Writer's Book*, ed. Helen Hull (New York: Barnes & Noble, 1956), pp. 38–39

**DAVID LITTLEJOHN**      Mrs. Petry has—this first must be granted—an uncomfortable tendency to contrive sordid plots (as opposed to merely writing of sordid events). She seems to require a "shocking" chain of scandalous doings, secret affairs, family skeletons revealed, brutal crimes, whispered evil, adulterous intrigue on which to cast her creative imagination, in the manner of the great Victorians or the tawdry moderns. So wise is her writing, though, so real are her characters, so total is her sympathy, that one can often accept the faintly cheap horrors and contrivances. Even if not, though, he can dispense with them. It may seem odd to suggest reading a novel while skipping the plot; but it can be done. And if one allows himself to be overexcited by these intrigues (it *is* hard to escape their clutches, but one should), he misses, I think, the real treasures of Ann Petry's fiction.

There is, first, more intelligence in her novels, paragraph for paragraph, than in those of any other writer I have mentioned; solid, earned, tested intelligence. This woman is sharp. Her wisdom is more useful, even, more durable, than the brilliant, diamond-edged acuteness of Gwendolyn Brooks.

This wisdom, secondly, reveals itself in a prose that is rich and crisp, and suavely shot with the metallic threads of irony. It is a style of constant surprise and delight, alive and alight on the page. It is so charged with sense and pleasure you can taste it—and yet never (almost never) is it mere "display."

And out of the female wisdom, the chewy style, grow characters of shape and dimension, people made out of love, with whole histories evoked in a page. There is not one writer in a thousand who owns so genuine and generous and undiscriminating a creative sympathy. Ann Petry *becomes* each character she mentions, grants each one a full, felt intensity of being, the mean and the loving, the white and the black, even when they come and go in only fifty words. ⟨. . .⟩

This, to me, the intelligence, the style, and above all the creative sympathy, is what sets Ann Petry apart from this second rank of American Negro novelists, sets her, in fact, into a place almost as prominent and promising as that of the bigger three. She is not, of course, writing "about" the race war, any more than most of the last eight or ten novelists mentioned are. This is a delusion fostered either by publishers, playing up a profitable approach, or by the fake guilty egocentricity of white readers, who presume that all books by Negroes must somehow be about them. But if an American Negro can, despite all, develop such an understanding of other people as

Ann Petry's—and more prodigious still, *convey* that understanding—then let her write what *Peyton Place*-plots she will, she is working toward a genuine truce in the war.

David Littlejohn, *Black on White: A Critical Survey of Writing by American Negroes* (New York: Grossman Publishers, 1966), pp. 154–56

---

**ALFRED KAZIN**      By contrast with Mr. ⟨Henry⟩ Van Dyke and/or the majority of black novelists, Ann Petry seems old-fashioned, so surprisingly "slow" in her narrative rhythm that you wonder if the title story in *Miss Muriel and Other Stories* took place in another century. Mrs. Petry's timing is as different from most contemporary black writing as is her locale, which in the best of these leisurely paced stories is a small upstate New York town where a pharmacist and his family are the only Negroes. Their life centers entirely around the drugstore itself. The longest and most successful of these stories, "Miss Muriel," tells of an eccentric elderly white shoemaker in the town, Mr. Bemish, who, to the astonishment and terror of the Negro family, falls in love with Aunt Sophronia. There is no "Muriel" in the story; the title is a sad joke about an old Negro who asked for "Muriel" cigars and was sternly told that *he* would have to ask for them as "Miss Muriel." But the feeling behind the "joke" is so strong in the small, isolated black family that poor Mr. Bemish not only doesn't get Aunt Sophronia, but is driven out of town for falling in love with a black lady.

This reversal of roles is typical of Mrs. Petry's quiet, always underplayed but deeply felt sense of situation. The other stories aren't as lovingly worked out as "Miss Muriel"—which is an artful period piece that brings back a now legendary age of innocence in white-black relationships. Several stories are just tragic situations that are meant to touch you by that quality alone. A famous black drummer loses his adored wife to a pianist in his band, but the drumming must go on; a Harlem old-clothes man falls in love with the oversized statue of a dark woman he calls "Mother Africa"; a Negro teacher is unable to stand up to a gang of young students and flees town, ashamed of not having played a more heroic part; a Negro woman at a convention is insulted by a white woman, and realizes in the morning, on learning that the other woman died of a heart attack during the night, that she might have saved her. These delicate points are characteristic of Mrs. Petry's quietly firm interest in fiction as moral dilemma. Clearly, her sense of the

Negro situation is still "tragic." Her stories are very far from contemporary black nationalist writing, and by no means necessarily more interesting. But they are certainly different.

Alfred Kazin, "Brothers Crying Out for More Access to Life," *Saturday Review*, 2 October 1971, pp. 34–35

**MARGARET B. McDOWELL**      As in all her work, Petry excels in *The Narrows* in her use of concrete detail, her ability to dramatize a situation, and her ear for exact dialogue. She is a master at transcribing the details of a given milieu as she recreates, for example, the sound of the river lapping against the dock at night, the feeling that fog generates as it rolls up the street from the river, the smell of beer from the saloon across from Abbie's brick house, and the glare of sunlight on the River Wye. To help convey the sense of plenitude in the social scene that she recreates in her novel, she appeals to the auditory sense of her reader, as when Mamie Powther sings her plaintive blues throughout the novel.

Each place, object, and fragment of dialogue becomes important in creating the realistic milieu, but certain aspects of the Narrows generate abstract associations. The cemetery becomes segregated, as if the dead must not mingle across racial lines. A myriad of placards proclaiming rooms for rent and a growing number of drifters sleeping under Abbie's big tree suggest the increasingly transient nature of the population. The River Wye, though a beautiful stream, draws the desperate to suicide. In its growing pollution, the river symbolizes, to a degree, the economic exploitation of the area. The naming of the Last Chance saloon promises fellowship as well as food and drink for the survival of the down-and-outer, but the name also implies an impending finality to those who need more than food and drink. It offers no further opportunities for the repressed of society to attain for themselves security, love or justice. Its neon sign is ugly and cheap, its owner's temper flares in murderous violence, and it is linked with lucrative prostitution and gambling enterprises which exploit the poor while providing them with specious pleasure. The Treadway estate—remote from the Narrows—is also symbolic. It is the site for an annual festival for the workers in a munitions plant, but the celebration is an impersonal gesture which expresses no true concern of the employers for their workers. The laborers, in turn, gossip viciously about Camilla Treadway's presence on the dock at Dumble Street at midnight when she was allegedly threatened with rape.

The motor cars of the Treadways—the Rolls-Royce and their fleet of Cadillacs—are symbolic of power. Camilla's automobiles make possible the anonymity which she and Link achieve by driving to Harlem. Camilla's impulsive, reckless driving suggests her instability. Treadway automobiles, in a more sinister context, facilitate the kidnaping of Link and the hauling away of his body. Bill Hod's secondhand Cadillacs represent the rewards of his shady dealings, many of which exploit his Black brothers and sisters, while F. K. Jackson's funeral limousine (with its whiskey bottle for the weary and its case of long black gloves and lace veil, available for any bereaved woman to wear for a half hour of proper mourning) reflects how superficial and conventional the rites of grief are to the capitalist entrepreneur.

> Margaret B. McDowell, "*The Narrows*: A Fuller View of Ann Petry," *Black American Literature Forum* 14, No. 4 (Winter 1980): 137

---

**BERNARD W. BELL**     Petry, like Himes and Wright, is adept at character delineation, but her protagonists are cut from a different cloth than those of her major contemporaries. Rather than sharing the pathology of a Bigger Thomas or Bob Jones or Lee Gordon, Lutie Johnson and Link Williams are intelligent, commonplace, middle-class aspiring blacks, who, despite the socialized ambivalence resulting from racism and economic exploitation, are not consumed by fear and hatred and rage. Petry's vision of black personality is not only different from that of Himes and Wright, but it is also more faithful to the complexities and varieties of black women, whether they are big-city characters like Mrs. Hedges in *The Street* or small-town characters like Abbie Crunch in *The Narrows*. Ann Petry thus moves beyond the naturalistic vision of Himes and Wright to a demythologizing of American culture and Afro-American character.

> Bernard W. Bell, "Ann Petry's Demythologizing of American Culture and Afro-American Character," *Conjuring: Black Women, Fiction, and Literary Tradition*, ed. Marjorie Pryse and Hortense J. Spillers (Bloomington: Indiana University Press, 1985), p. 114

---

**JAMES DE JONGH**     Ann Petry's *The Street* (1943), Ralph Ellison's *Invisible Man* (1952), and James Baldwin's *Go Tell It on the Mountain* (1952)

⟨. . .⟩ are the three novels of this period to rise above typical expression of the emerging ghetto and incorporate the new Harlem of the 1930s and 1940s with transcendent and enduring literary artistry. *The Street* is a keenly observed portrait of the emerging ghetto of Harlem in the early 1940s, and a vivid perceptual rendering as well. The omniscient narrator of *The Street* identifies so convincingly with the perspective of the particular character from whose point of view each specific portion of the story is told that the illusion of a flow of intimate, overlapping autobiographies is sustained without compromising the impartial authority of the narrative voice. Consequently, Petry's third-person narrative reads with the intimacy and perceptual emphasis of a first-person narration. ⟨. . .⟩ Perceptual interpretation of Harlem in *The Street* is reserved almost exclusively for Lutie Johnson, the novel's protagonist. Lutie's view of Harlem is the one that counts in *The Street*, for her struggle to rebuild her family is waged against the malevolent phenomenon of Harlem itself. The microcosmic form of one block of 116th Street is a personage in its own right, and Lutie's true antagonist. ⟨. . .⟩

Lutie tries to make money with her modest voice, when Boots, a Harlem bandleader, is attracted to her. She is unaware that the bandleader is himself little more than a pawn of the malevolent forces of Harlem, embodied by Mrs. Hedges and Junto, two benignly placid puppetmasters whose bizarre relationship constitutes one of the most inventive details in *The Street*. Mrs. Hedges is a gigantic black woman, whose scars from a fire confine her to a comfortably furnished first-floor apartment in the building to which Lutie moves. Junto is a physically unprepossessing white man, who first ran across Mrs. Hedges when he was starting out as a junk dealer in Harlem and recognized her to be one of the few people of any race with a "self-will" comparable to his own. Junto is not squeamish in any way about Mrs. Hedges's scarred and unwomanly figure. To him, she is uniquely attractive, but her own sensitivity about her appearance has made any physical intimacy impossible. Instead Junto and Mrs. Hedges have sublimated their intense feelings into a curious business relationship. From her apartment in a building owned by Junto, Mrs. Hedges has spent her time looking at the life of the street and, with the insights gained from ceaseless observation, has directed Junto to the best investments in Harlem—places where people dance, drink, and make love, in order to forget their troubles. Together the couple monopolize a substantial portion of Harlem's infrastructure, each profiting in respective ways from Harlem by pacifying the pain of the very oppressions that they conspire to create and sustain. His bar, called the Junto, creates an oasis of warmth in winter and of coolness in summer by giving black men the illusion of dignity and younger black women the illusion of possessing the fine things they lack. One of Mrs. Hedges's few pleasures is presenting beautiful, compliant young black women to Junto as symbolic substitutes for herself. After he tires of each stand-in, Junto sets the woman up in one of his classier houses for white clients, and Mrs. Hedges offers up another surrogate to their odd passion. For much of the novel, Lutie is the unwitting target of this bizarrely touching relationship. Mrs. Hedges identifies Lutie for such a role early in the novel and is content to watch and wait, defending Lutie from physical harm while secretly using Harlem to break Lutie's spirit. Only gradually, as circumstances conspire to force her to submit, does Lutie begin to understand that Harlem and Junto are facets of each other. Junto makes Harlem bearable, while Harlem makes the Junto indispensable and profitable. Harlem has become less an instrument of black hopes and aspirations, and more a means of limiting and controlling blacks. As Junto's net closes around her, Lutie kills in desperation and flees Harlem in despair, abandoning the young son whose future was the principal motivation for her struggle with life on the street in the first place.

James de Jongh, *Vicious Modernism: Black Harlem and the Literary Imagination* (New York: Cambridge University Press, 1990), pp. 89–92

---

**DIANNE JOHNSON**     A particularly distinguished historical novel is *Tituba of Salem Village*. Set in Salem Village, Massachusetts in 1692, this historical fiction recreates some of the events surrounding and leading up to the infamous Salem witch trials. More specifically, it recreates the story of Tituba Indian, a slave brought to Massachusetts from Barbados, who was one of the first three women to be condemned as being a "witch." What she is, in reality, is an artist, though she is not a singer, or painter, or writer. But she does have talent, which she hones, which she perfects and practices, and which is misinterpreted and misunderstood. She is, in fact, a master of herbal medicine and the art of healing.

Petry meticulously includes details which inform this particular world view, a world view in which Tituba is nurtured and of which she is and always remains a part. The first clue that the reader has that Tituba is part of a non-western world is when the narrator talks about the thunderstone that was given to her by an old man:

As long as she kept it with her, she would have a part of the
island with her. The old man who had given it to her had told
her that if she ever thought her life was in danger, she was to
unwrap the thunderstone and hold it in her hand. If she felt it
move in her hand, it was a sign that she would live. She wasn't
sure that she believed this, but she wouldn't want to lose the
thunderstone.

This last sentence is crucial. In effect, the second half negates the doubt
expressed in the first half. Tituba is, in fact, entrenched in this particular
culture. ⟨. . .⟩

⟨. . .⟩ Lillian Smith asserts that "historical fiction must be a fusion of
story and period if it is to enrich and enlarge our picture of the past to the
extent that it becomes part of our experience." And this is precisely what
Petry accomplishes. She powerfully draws the interconnectedness between
color, one's identity (servants referred to as Black first, then by name),
religion, culture, and historical era. I have focused here on African/Black
characters. But in fact, their blackness in and of itself is not the single
focal point of the novel. On the other hand, their blackness is an integral
component of their very beings. And in recreating their stories, in their
respective and particular time periods, the author integrates this into a
composite portrait.

> Dianne Johnson, *Telling Tales: The Pedagogy and Promise of African American Literature
> for Youth* (Westport, CT: Greenwood Press, 1990), pp. 53–55

---

**NELLIE Y. McKAY**     In addition to its focus on a female protagonist,
*The Street* is significantly different from its male counterparts in that while
Petry lashes out uncompromisingly at racism, classism, and sexism, she
undercuts the conventions of the naturalistic novel by refusing to make
Lutie a mere victim of her social environment. Nor does this step on the
part of the author lessen the impact of the oppression of that environment.
Lutie may well have had greater success in achieving her goals had she
been less innocent of the politics of race, class, and gender. Her uncritical
acceptance of white middle-class values and the capitalist tenets of the
American dream make her an easy prey for the greed and sexism of the
black and white men who surround her. In addition, Lutie serves herself
poorly by separating from any support she might have had from the black

community and those values that have insured black survival in America since the first slaves arrived on its shores. Preoccupied with her ambitions for herself and her son to escape the poverty and disillusionment of black ghetto life and wholly uncritical of the white models to which she is exposed, she has no friends or relatives with whom she seeks association, attends no church, and in her attitudes, denies the possibilities of communal sources of strength. Consequently, she was vulnerable to the greed, anger, and sexism of those who were capable of destroying her.

> Nellie Y. McKay, "Ann Petry's *The Street* and *The Narrows*: A Study of the Influence of Class, Race, and Gender on Afro-American Women's Lives," *Women and War: The Changing Status of American Women from the 1930s to the 1950s*, ed. Maria Diedrich and Dorothea Fischer-Hornung (New York: Berg, 1990), pp. 134–35

---

**KEITH CLARK**      While something of an anachronism in the 1990s, the African-American protest novel of the 1940s and 1950s maintained a symbiotic relationship with the mythic American Dream: It decried a history of American racism which made achieving the Dream a chimera for blacks. While Richard Wright is considered the "father" of the genre, and *Native Son* (1940) its quintessential document, Ann Petry emerged as another strident voice—a progenitor or native daughter. While her novel *The Narrows* (1953) deviated somewhat, it nevertheless continued the Wrightian tradition. Link Williams, the protagonist, differs superficially from Bigger in that he has attained a Dartmouth education and enjoys relative freedom from economic hardships; it would *appear* that he has the means to acquire the bootstraps over which Bigger can only ruminate. However, Link's "success" cannot shield him in an America which insists upon his inhumanity. When he breaks the taboos of class and race by having an affair with a white New England heiress, his violent murder becomes ritual—an inexorable response to a black stepping out of his "place." While Petry's "New England" novel echoes *Native Son* thematically, more ostensibly it also foregrounds the black *male* as the victim of an America which denies African-Americans their very personhood. But in *The Street* (1946), Petry recasts the Herculean quest for the American Dream in an unequivocally female context. Indeed, the novel represents the "distaff" side of the African-American literary tradition, emerging as a groundbreaking work in its examination of the black women's pursuit of happiness. Not only does Petry depict how women pursue the Dream in traditionally "American" terms, but, more deftly, she illustrates how black women subvert the quest for the American Dream and fulfill their own version of it.

Given the spurious nature of the American Dream, one would assume that the African-American writer would vigorously expose its shortcomings—for instance, the myopic measuring of "success" in monetary and material terms. But the tendency has not been so much to attack the Dream as to *protest* whites' insistence on treating blacks as outsiders and interlopers. Indeed, the hue and cry of the Biggers and the Walter Lee Youngers emanate from their staunch loyalty to the hallowed Constitution, which stipulates that "all men are created equal"; they cry only because they want their slice of the pie. As Richard Yarborough points out, "Despite severe disappointments, . . . Afro-Americans have generally been among the most fervent believers in the American Dream."

Lutie Johnson, the protagonist in *The Street*, embodies the female version of the archetypal quest. Patterning her life after Benjamin Franklin's, Lutie embarks on an expedition she hopes will bestow the trappings of success upon herself and Bub, her eight-year-old son. However, Lutie's odyssey from Jamaica, New York, to Lyme, Connecticut, to Harlem bestows upon her little more than disillusionment. Ultimately, what Calvin Hernton calls the "three isms"—racism, capitalism and sexism—launch an implacable assault on Lutie, precipitating the novel's tragic conclusion.

While it would be tempting to view the novel as a treatise on how men, black and white, collude to destroy the All-American black girl, Petry's text discourages this sort of naturalistic preoccupation with character as subject and object. Instead, one might view this seminal examination of the black woman's search for the Dream as a mosaic—much like Alice Walker's tropological quilt—that includes other women, other stories, and other voices. In addition to presenting Lutie and her blind adherence to American values, Petry depicts two black female characters who circumvent the quest: Mrs. Hedges, who operates a bordello in the apartment building where Lutie lives and who also oversees the day-to-day events on "the street," and Min, the downtrodden and subservient companion of William Jones, the building superintendent.

Far from being minor characters, Mrs. Hedges and Min embody what I see as a history of black women *subverting* the vacuous Dream myth through an almost innate ability to secure their own space despite the twin scourges of racism and sexism. Existing in a milieu where the Dream's core assumptions belie their lived realities, these black women *undermine* the myth, altering it to ensure both economic survival and varying degrees of emotional stability. And because "traditional" principles have been the bane of black people since America's inception, questions involving "morality" of how these women survive become ancillary ones given their predatory, hostile environment.

Superficially, Mrs. Hedges and Min adhere to the ideals of "hard work" and "ingenuity" in a country where "anything is possible." However, these women more accurately replicate techniques used by such archetypal African-American trickster figures as Charles Chesnutt's Uncle Julius or black folklore's Peetie Wheatstraw in (re)inventing lives independent of the white American Dream. While denied opulent lifestyles and material objects, Petry's "minor" women attain life's basic necessities, and, given their tenuous existences, they (re)construct their own "dream" by tapping into a tradition of what Peter Wheatstraw in *Invisible Man* calls " 'shit, grit and mother-wit.' " Thus, *The Street* transcends the boundaries of the *"roman-à-these,"* the thesis presumably being that white racism extinguishes all black hope. The denizens of Petry's Harlem face a world more Darwinian than Franklinian, and they act according to their individual circumstances.

Keith Clark, "A Distaff Dream Deferred? Ann Petry and the Art of Subversion," *African American Review* 26, No. 3 (Fall 1992): 495–97

# ▣ Bibliography

*The Street.* 1946.

*Country Place.* 1947.

*The Drugstore Cat.* 1949.

*The Narrows.* 1953.

*Harriet Tubman, Conductor on the Underground Railroad.* 1955.

*Tituba of Salem Village.* 1964.

*The Common Ground: A Talk Given at the Central Children's Room of the New York Public Library.* c. 1964.

*Legends of the Saints.* 1970.

*Miss Muriel and Other Stories.* 1971.

# John A. Williams
## b. 1925

JOHN A. WILLIAMS was born in Jacksonville, Mississippi, on December 5, 1925. He was raised in Syracuse, New York, however, thereby avoiding the thriving racism of the South. Williams confronted this type of racism, though, after enlisting in the navy in 1943. Black soldiers, usually in segregated units, sailed off to fight for the American ideals of democracy and freedom, ideals that were hardly realized for blacks in America. This irony is captured in Williams's novel *Captain Blackman* (1972), in which he explores the role of black men in the American military.

After the war Williams returned to Syracuse. In 1947 he married Carolyn Clopton, with whom he had two sons. In 1950 he received a B.A. in journalism and English from Syracuse University. Two years later his marriage broke up and he turned to writing. Working for such magazines as *Ebony, Jet, Holiday,* and *Newsweek,* Williams enjoyed recognition as a successful journalist. He continued to write about racial inequality in his fiction. His first novel, *The Angry Ones* (1960), is somewhat autobiographical and examines the problems of relationships in general and interracial sex in particular.

*Night Song* (1961), Williams's second novel, was inspired largely by the life of the jazz artist Charlie "Bird" Parker. The work returns to the theme of sexual relations in a racially unequal world. In *Sissie* (1963) Williams illustrates how love can fall by the wayside in the struggle of black Americans for survival in a white world. Williams was moving toward an increasingly bleak view of relations between blacks and whites. In *The Man Who Cried I Am* (1967), which was well received by both critics and the public, he explores the black writer's conflict between being simply a man and being part of a group, namely the oppressed black minority. He also gives vent to the most extreme fears of black Americans—a white conspiracy to exterminate blacks.

Williams has been one of the most prolific of all black American writers. His later books such as *Mothersill and the Foxes* (1975) and *!Click Song*

(1982) focus more on his belief in the need for solidarity within the black community.

In 1965 Williams married Lorrain Isaac, with whom he had one son. He has held teaching positions at such institutions as the City College of New York, the University of California at Santa Barbara, and Boston University. Since 1979 he has been professor of English at Rutgers University (Newark campus).

Williams's predominant concern with race problems in America and the history of black Americans is also expressed in his works of nonfiction, such as *Africa: Her History, Lands and People* (1962) and *Minorities in the City* (1975). *This Is My Country Too* (1965) is an account of his journey through the United States on assignment for *Holiday* magazine. He has written biographies of Richard Wright, Martin Luther King, Jr., and Richard Pryor, edited the anthology *The Angry Black* (1962), and, with Gilbert H. Muller, compiled several anthologies of literature.

# ▧ *Critical Extracts*

**JOHN A. WILLIAMS**     Negro writers are nearly always compared to one another, rather than to white writers. This, like labeling and grouping, tends to limit severely the expansion of the talents of Negro writers and confine them to a literary ghetto from which only one Negro name at a time may emerge. Today it is unmistakably James Baldwin; no Negro writing in America today can escape his shadow. He replaced Richard Wright, who, in turn, may have replaced Langston Hughes.

Editors, too, have been guilty of labeling, comparing, and grouping. "Negro stuff is selling well!" I heard an editor say. So publishers have hastened to sign up Negro writers whose best qualification, often enough, was that they were Negro. Publishing has had its homosexual phase, which dies hard; its gray flannel-advertising phase, its war phase, its Jewish phase. It is now in its Negro phase. To illustrate shifting trends, six years ago an editor whose house is now the hottest because of its Negro talent, said, in essence, in a note to my agent (which was passed on to me—a sign of how grim the business of selling "Negro" books was) that it would be wiser if I were to set aside the obviously personal experiences of being Negro. Financially at least, the change in his point of view has been good for him.

The current trend toward more publishing of books by Negro authors, brought about by national considerations, has been beneficial to black writers. Nevertheless, much comparison of their work still exists in the editorial offices. This comes from my files; it is part of a report, dated seven years ago, on a book that I have since published elsewhere: "Mr. Williams is in the vein of Chester Himes, and to my mind achieves a similar power."

Excluding riding the trend, the other attitudes—labeling, grouping, and comparing—provide the biggest block to the expansion by Negro writers of themes and techniques (cared for so little by reviewers today). Perhaps that is the reason for the existence of these attitudes. They are automatic and no one thinks about them except Negro writers. Either consciously or unconsciously, this kind of bigotry tells more about the reviewer than it does about the book he's reviewing.

John A. Williams, "The Literary Ghetto," *Saturday Review*, 20 April 1963, pp. 21, 40

---

**RONALD WALCOTT**        *The Man Who Cried I Am* may be read as the chronicle of Max Reddick's political education, witness to his transformation from petit bourgeois to dispenser of a document of so monumental a political revelation that its very possession insures one's death. Counterposed to the imminence of death, indeed the obsession with death, political and personal, which haunts the novel from its first pages, however, is the fact that the tale told is very much concerned with life, with survival—its possibility, the terms by which it can be negotiated, the pain and diminution of the self that are inherent aspects of the self's struggle to survive. It is a story of life struggling to emerge from the shroud of death, from all those forces that conspire to thwart it.

The novel opens with an image which will stay with it to the end, an image of a man dying. Senses only half-deadened by alcohol, librium and morphine, Max Reddick, middle-aged novelist, acknowledged "success," reporter, fool, innocent, a man consumed by a terminal cancer of the rectum, is sitting in a street cafe in Amsterdam waiting for his ex-wife, Margrit, to arrive so that he can "tell her why it (the marriage) hadn't worked," or more precisely, why he had felt compelled to bring on its death (supposedly to spare her the pain of watching him die). Indeed, he is in Europe because of death, because his friend Harry Ames had died. Before Ames is finished dealing with him from beyond the grave, Reddick will be dead also, the joke, if one can accept it as such, being that Reddick is a walking dead man anyway. Asked by Ames' mistress, what is wrong? Reddick replies, "What is wrong with me is what is wrong with all of us. I'm simply dying. Like you. Like everybody."

What matters here as elsewhere is the manner of dying. Reddick's walking death is ghastly, the offensive details of which are treated with a grisly attention and obsessive force: the stink of death is about him; when he urinates, he urinates blood; as he bathes the water turns to "pinkish color"; riding in a car blood soaks his clothing; in the cafe he hears the "squish" of his raging rectum; to make love would be to commit suicide. So insistently does the novel dwell on these details that it becomes clear Reddick's is by no means a physical cancer only. His decomposition is society's: it is the cancer of race in America; more than that, his decay is emblematic of the social decomposition of the times. It is, in short, the beginning of a metaphor which will encompass the world.

Ronald Walcott, "The Man Who Cried I Am: Crying in the Dark," Studies in Black Literature 3, No. 1 (Spring 1972): 25–26

---

**RONALD WALCOTT**    The search motif that pervades his fiction is also the dominant motif, and motive, of *This Is My Country, Too*, the chronicle of Williams' journey through America on assignment for *Holiday* magazine.

Shortly after the publication of *Sissie*, in 1963, Williams "set out in search of an old dream, one that faded and came back and faded again. The search was for my America." The opportunity for this search was occasioned by a request from *Holiday* magazine for a series of "travel" essays in which he was "to drive around the country and see and listen to Americans. I was to take the pulse of the country as nearly as I could." The assignment in September of 1963 was to have a significant effect on his developing political thought and on the thematic conceptions of his fiction, as well as deepening and making more ironic the continuing search motif begun in his first work, *The Angry Ones*, in which Steve Hill, also driving around the country, travels three thousand miles from Los Angeles to New York, "running, feeling that oblique hunger for a thing I didn't even know." ⟨. . .⟩

With one important surprise: the majority of his experiences corroborated his early assumption that America was indeed undergoing an agonizing but very real period of social transformation. "I searched and came away with hope." This was 1963.

One year after the *Holiday* assignment, Williams affixed an epilog to the book for its paperback reissue in which he grimly discusses the conclusions he "had to reach" on the basis of his travels: namely, that "man as I knew him best, in America, was not basically good, as is always suggested, but evil in the primitive, offensive and destructive sense." Offering a précis of American history in which he points to our criminal beginnings as "thieves, and murderers, many of us," Williams notes that the logical conclusion of this is that "We were born of violence," a fact which "does explain not only our own history but that of the world."

Ronald Walcott, "The Early Fiction of John A. Williams," CLA Journal 16, No. 2 (December 1972): 200–201

---

**WILLIAM M. BURKE**    The novel's ultimate affirmation, as the title ⟨The Man Who Cried I Am⟩ implies, is based on Max's resistance to a world controlled by power rather than justice, since such a world would deny the values of his own life. When Max works to defeat the Alliance Blanc, he is responding to a deep and positive conviction about the worth of life. His reflection on his past life reveals not only cyclical patterns of cruelty and bloodshed, but consistent patterns of nobility and compassion. Whatever instinct drives men to destruction of one another, another instinct creates bonds between them. Small acts of heroism stand out among great acts of deception. Love and compassion between men and women stand in opposition to the hatred at loose in the world. Max and Margrit, for example, manage some precious moments in their relationship, and their mutual waiting for each other at the cafe table at the beginning and end of the novel suggests the endurance of their love. Even the suffering that Max experiences from his tumor is a private acknowledgment of worth because it certifies his existence: "He was bored with New Deals and Square Deals and New Frontiers and Great Societies; suspicious of the future, untrusting of the past. He was sure of one thing: that he was; that he existed. The pain in his ass told him so." He hurts; therefore he is. Although affected by great social movements, he is able to view his private consciousness as separate from them: his awareness is a unique, special, and concrete event. From somewhere in the depths of that awareness Max is able to cry *I am* against the dehumanizing and oppressing forces of history, human nature, politics, and racism.

> William M. Burke, "The Resistance of John A. Williams: *The Man Who Cried I Am*," *Critique* 15, No. 3 (1973): 11

**NOEL SCHRAUFNAGEL**     In *Sissie* (1963) Williams concentrates on illustrating the malicious effects of a ghetto environment on a famous black entertainer. The novel stresses the point that a childhood spent in a ghetto leaves a lasting impression on an individual. In the case of Iris Joplin, the bitter memories of poverty, discrimination, and the constant battle between her parents, have affected her to the point that life in America is impossible. She is unable, in fact, to forgive her dying mother for the treatment she received as a child, although the old woman herself is primarily a victim of her environment.

Iris, and her brother Ralph, return to their home in California where Sissie, the mother, is on her deathbed. Iris, a famed European singer, and Ralph, an American playwright, discuss their early life during the process of their journey home. Iris is infuriated by the kind of life Sissie and her husband, Big Ralph, led. The problems associated with the unemployed male in combat with the black matriarch were intensified by Big Ralph's tendency to drink and carouse. The consequent hardship placed on the children alienated Iris from her parents, and her bitterness persists. Young Ralph also has suffered greatly from the depravity of his youth and the racial incidents that have occurred over the years, but he is able to forgive his parents to a large degree as he realizes that white oppression is the main reason for their failures. Sissie, meanwhile, reflects on her past life as she awaits the arrival of her children, and death. Her husband had at one time been a promising young man but he was unable to cope with a society that denied him his masculinity. His compensatory devices created tensions in the family that were never resolved. As Iris and her brother arrive at Sissie's side the drama centers on whether Iris will forgive her mother. Iris' mind has been corrupted by the years of hatred and self-pity, though, and Sissie dies with the wrath of her daughter still upon her.

While the anger of Iris is directed at her mother, it is the racism of American society that is basically responsible for Iris' perverted views. Sissie and her son, Ralph, are strong enough to withstand the environment and oppression, bur Iris and Big Ralph succumb to the pressures in their own way. Iris sympathizes to some extent with her emasculated father. Sissie is the object of her hate largely because Iris blames her for Big Ralph's impotency, but Sissie was merely fulfilling the role that was passed on to her by the dictates of a society in which the black male tends to be denied his manhood. The obtuse Iris fails to realize the true situation, for racism, compounded by her own shortcomings, has destroyed her vision. *Sissie* lacks the poignancy of *Night Song,* though, as Williams places a heavy emphasis on the propagandistic elements of the novel without a concomitant artistic development. He belabors the theme of oppression to the extent that his style is not capable of supporting it without resorting to diatribe.

Noel Schraufnagel, *From Apology to Protest: The Black American Novel* (Deland, FL: Everett/Edwards, 1973), pp. 150–51

---

**CLARENCE MAJOR**     Williams's struggle before luck came was long and rigorous. He was a working writer for many years before his first book was published. Certainly, more than five years before his first novel, *The Angry Ones,* was published in 1960, he was sending book manuscripts to publishers who were rejecting them, almost always for the wrong reasons. So when in 1963 he found reviewers grouping his novel, *Sissie,* together with new works by, say, James Baldwin and John Oliver Killens, his disapproval was understandable. He was also aware that almost nobody except black writers thought or cared about this fact, which might well be thoughtless bigotry on the part of the reviewer.

From the beginning Williams much admired Chester Himes, a prolific writer of many novels in the naturalistic tradition which Williams himself followed. He also admired Richard Wright of whom he wrote: "Many black writers were influenced by Richard Wright, and this, too, I believe, is the sign of an artist, that he is in many ways emulated; the power of his words or the color of his canvas impel others toward their own palettes or pens." And on one of Wright's books he says "I found *Pagan Spain* to be one of

Wright's most perceptive books . . . Wright had no particular stake in Spain except as a human being interested in the plight of other human beings. This marked a very special growth all black writers must move toward—from the burning consideration of the black oppressed to the final consideration of *all* oppressed peoples. In the final analysis, it is this consideration that makes Wright the most important black writer, American, of all times."

Williams himself chose to write novels because they allowed the writer to "explore vigorously the endless delights and agonies . . . only the novel approaches the grandeur, the sweep, the universality of the epic poem." He continued to feel this way as year by year it grew more obvious that the reading public was turning away from fiction toward nonfiction.

Though Williams proved himself early to be an expert short story writer, he considered such writing to be mainly a "training ground for the novelist."

> Clarence Major, "John A. Williams: The Black Writer Who Cried I Am," *The Dark and Feeling* (New York: Third Press, 1974), pp. 86–87

**ROGER ROSENBLATT**      The idea that one day all black men and women may suddenly disappear, either from a certain region or from the face of the earth, has recurred quite often in black writing. In the satire *Black No More* (1931), George Schuyler conceived of a plot in which the "Negro Problem" was solved by "electrical nutrition," a process which changed the texture of the hair, the skin color, and other facial features of black people, thereby making them all white, and disturbing the racial balance of the nations. ⟨William Melvin⟩ Kelley's *A Different Drummer* describes a State of the Union from which all blacks depart. Douglas Turner Ward's *Day of Absence* is a play about the same subject: the disappearance of blacks from a Southern town and the ensuing effects on the white population. In Williams' *The Man Who Cried I Am*, Max uncovers an international conspiracy to systematically eliminate the black people of the world.

The different treatments of this theme range from the grim to the hilarious, but each of them is inspired in part by the fear that the disappearance of black Americans is a desirable notion to whites, and that by means of assimilation, isolation, or destruction, it may one day come to pass. The theme is also informed by the fact that most white people do not recognize blacks, do not see them as people. Paradoxically, blacks who wish to be seen by such whites often have to "turn white" or colorless in order to be seen, thereby performing a disappearing act of their own. To evoke literary situations in which black people disappear, then, is a statement of a kind of inner reality despite the seeming exaggeration of the proposition. Moreover, at one point or another almost every black hero seeks to escape from his rut or corner by vanishing, and so becomes an accomplice in his own elimination.

> Roger Rosenblatt, *Black Fiction* (Cambridge, MA: Harvard University Press, 1974), pp. 184–85

**JERRY H. BRYANT**     *The Man Who Cried I Am* is in a sense Williams's *Huckleberry Finn*. It reflects his deep skepticism over the capacity of America to live up to its professed ideals, and a development of deep pessimism about whites in particular and man in general. The intensity of its melancholy demonstrates the strength of Williams's emotional attachment to America. The gloom that the novel conveys is the result of seeing that one's most optimistic convictions are laid in sand, and that the building of the pure ideal was doomed from the start. ⟨. . .⟩

The black writer can have no subject but America and Americans, as Harry Ames tells Max. The artist cannot abandon to the politicians the issues of the race question; they are too important to be subjected to political over-simplification. Furthermore, they constitute the truly valid material the artist has to work with. Thus, the question for Williams is not whether the novelist shall be political, but how shall he be so? His answer is that the black novelist uses his art to transform America and the black person through understanding. He cannot afford to forget the danger, fear, and hate in America nor can he afford to forget, as he says in *This Is My Country Too*, "much love" and "goodwill." Williams's last three novels suggest that he has modified the optimism of that statement, made in 1964. Williams continues writing novels trying to warn whites and encourage blacks, appealing to reason and good will, sometimes fear and nationalism. That in itself is an act of faith in the potential of white Americans eventually to implement their Creed and of black Americans to help them do it. Williams suggests that the black novelist has greater stake in this effort than the white. As a descendent of those original slaves who survived at all costs, he "is committed to the search, the hope, the challenge, whether I want to be or not, for America has yet to sing its greatest song."

Jerry H. Bryant, "John A. Williams: The Political Use of the Novel," *Critique* 16, No. 3 (1975): 99–100

**C. LYNN MUNROE**     Williams's efforts to unpack the myths which contribute to the marginality of the black American are evident in his first novel, *The Angry Ones*, which functions largely as an imaginative rendering of his own initial encounters with the American mythology. Although lacking the necessary distance to make this a great book, Williams manages to initiate the reader into the world of the black professional, to explore both its motivations and frustrations and to consider the available alternatives from several points of view.

The book revolves around Steve Hill's quest to survive despite his economic and social vulnerability. On the rebound from a luckless search for publicity work in California, Steve returns to New York and is again subjected to discrimination in hiring and housing. As in his later works, Williams introduces a confidant, Obie Robertson, as a foil against which to play Steve's perceptions of his situation. Although he finished first in his class, Obie, too, is confined to marginal employment. Through his protrayal of Obie's decline, Williams is able to examine the manner in which the personality is brutalized by an unaccepting environment.

While nothing cataclysmic befalls Steve in his daily encounters with the often blatant racism of American society, Williams is quick to reveal the toll which living with repressed anger and the imminent threat of violence exact upon the individual and his relationships. Steve's struggle is both internal and external. He, like his parents, had at one time believed that "education would make us free," but has gradually realized that degrees mean little if one is black. He finally secures employment with Rocket publishers, a vanity house which is the quintessence of the American dream. Ostensibly, it allows everyone a chance to achieve fame and fortune; in reality, it exploits people's dreams for profit.

C. Lynn Munroe, "Culture and Quest in the Fiction of John A. Williams," *CLA Journal* 22, No. 2 (December 1978): 74

**JOHN M. REILLY**      While some of the first reviewers of *The Outsider* ⟨by Richard Wright⟩ noticed its kinship with the thriller, they, like most subsequent readers and critics, found the expository and didactic prupose of the novel so ponderous as to bury the significance of generic innovation. Quite the opposite is the case for readers of John A. Williams's remarkable adaptation of the historical mode of fiction in *Captain Blackman* (1972). Through the device of a corporate hero, who relives the military history of Black American soldiers, Williams both repudiates the individualist premise of the novel and fulfills the latent possibility of a truly popular historical fiction. The first task is accomplished by placing Abraham Blackman within realistically detailed episodes involving Black soldiers from the battles of Lexington and Concord, through Andrew Jackson's victory at New Orleans, the Civil War, the Indian wars, and the foreign military adventures of the United States from 1898 to Viet Nam. In all of these engagements Abraham Blackman, the incarnation of the Black fighting man, is sensitive to the importance of his historical position, first as one fighting to earn his manumission through national service and later as a member of America's colonial battalions deployed against other colonials. Blackman is a figure particularized by Williams's provision of a biography for him that includes the personal feelings of love, frustration, and ambition, but, as his name insists, he is equally a figure typifying the collective enterprise of Blacks seeking participation in history as conscious actors. ⟨. . .⟩

If genres were fixed, authoritative types, Williams's excursion into fantasy-utopia would be inconsistent with his otherwise realistic novel. Disregarding the survival of benighted critics holding *a priori* conceptions of literary types, I conclude, however, that it is precisely the ending of *Captain Blackman* that completes its logic. Presenting the outcome of history in a version of fantasy, Williams jettisons the premise of realism—the assumption that verbal text reflects an objective reality. Instead, he presents his novel as a creation frankly governed by the artist's imagination, replacing the domination of an old genre with the new control of Black writer's consciousness. As in *12 Million Black Voices* and *The Outsider*, but more clearly than in the latter, the manner of writing in *Captain Blackman* constitutes shaping of narrative history.

John M. Reilly, "The Reconstruction of Genre as Entry into Conscious History," *Black American Literature Forum* 13, No. 1 (Spring 1979): 5–6

**WOLFGANG KARREL**      John A. Williams once complained that white critics tend to compare black writers only with other black writers, thus cementing segregation and double standards in criticism as in life. *Night Song* provides an excellent opportunity not only in technique or discourse but also in subject matter or story for a comparison with other fictional accounts of Charlie Parker who remains the most important influence in modern jazz and one of the greatest musicians the United States have produced. ⟨. . .⟩

The indirect presentation of Charlie Parker through a white mono- or multiperspective has a long tradition going back at least to "Sparrow's Last Jump." So has the theme of exploitive relations: Moe Alvin in *Night Song* owes as much to Harry McNeil as the critic Stanley Crane to Cortázar's Bruno. Hip talk, bohemia setting and interracial sex are also standard ingredients in the jazz novel. *Night Song* further depicts Parker in the tragic convention of a Christ in black face (Cortázar) or ritual scapegoat (Holmes). Williams' original contribution to the tradition lies in his foregrounding of the race question and in casting the "White Negro" or American beatnik in the Judas role. Thus *Night Song* appears as an implicit rejection and analysis of the beatnik's admiration for Charlie Parker and be bop life styles. The primitivism of his admirers is part of the same racism that destroyed Charlie Parker. Williams, however, still believes in the conversion of white liberals and—though far less optimistically than in *One of New York*—takes a cautious integrationist position. Integration cannot happen without white sacrifices. Della Madison has to obey Keel Robinson, and David Hillary fails Richie Stokes by not risking his position for him. This seemed a viable black statement in 1961 though it turned out to be the white students rather than the college professors or the beatniks who stood up to the challenge by joining the Civil Rights Movement.

There is another aspect in which *Night Song* might be considered representative of black fiction at the critical juncture between social-criticism traditions, Civil Rights Movement and Beat Generation. *Night Song* defines successful integration primarily in terms of interracial sex or, more precisely, in terms of the relation between a black man and a white woman. ⟨. . .⟩

*Night Song* seems to reflect where John A. Williams—and with him Baldwin, Smith and other black writers—stood in the early sixties. But it is also an example of the limitations audience and publishers imposed on black writers without any bargaining power. Social criticism, no longer marketable as "protest," had to be couched in literary conventions of

"Anger," "Beat," and the well-made novel of the Henry James type to be acceptable. The contradictions in *Night Song* also reflect the uneasy compromise of a young writer with the exigencies of the publishing market which it may have helped to change a little.

Wolfgang Karrel, "Multiperspective and the Hazards of Integration: John A. Williams' *Night Song*," *The Afro-American Novel Since 1960*, ed. Peter Bruck and Wolfgang Karrel (Amsterdam: B. R. Grüner, 1982), pp. 91, 96, 98

**GILBERT H. MULLER**     For John Williams, the territory ahead is no longer uncharted, although it might still hold surprises for him and for his expanding reading public. His personal and artistic worlds can never be apolitical, and thus the fiction of the future will continue to flesh out those points on the literary and historical map that have always been central to his vision: racism, exploitation, and oppression; characters on a collision course with history who seek nevertheless personal and political affirmations. In the meantime, Williams's visibility and prominence as a major writer and interpreter of the American scene continue to evolve slowly. The superlative presentation of a three-part television film based on *The Junior Bachelor Society*, aired in late September of 1981, brought a new dimension of success and recognition to its author. *!Click Song*, released in the spring of 1982, projects new strengths as well as a deeper, softer, and more reflective voice of the mature artist. His play, *Last Flight from Ambo Ber*, first offered in trial production in Boston, breaks new literary ground but is still political and historical in nature, covering a period of more than seventy-five years. ⟨. . .⟩

The novels of John Williams, which ultimately will be the measure of his stature as an artist, offer to us what Lionel Trilling termed "our sense of a culture's hum and buzz of implication . . . the whole evanescent context in which explicit statements are made." In both their uniqueness and commonality, the novels draw us together in a web of cultural and historical recognition. Williams wants us to learn something intense and powerful about American life from his work. And the hardships that we uncover in the fiction are balanced by the affirmations—the confirmation that in returning to ourselves and the basic values that make us human, we understand ourselves and the world better. Williams persistently has revealed the worst and tried to confirm the best aspects of our lives in the modern period.

This is his constant task, and one that he does not plan to abandon. For the circus is still going on, he declares, the tent never closes.

Gilbert H. Muller, *John A. Williams* (Boston: Twayne, 1984), pp. 154–55

**JOHN M. REILLY**     Williams conceived of *The Man Who Cried I Am* in a field of discourse on Black experience dominated by images of victimization, and typically requiring appeals and exhortations addressed to the conscience of white readers. Though Anglo-Saxon racial argument has been diminished in the novel to presupposition clothed, as by the King Alfred Plan, in the garments of *Realpolitik*, Williams addresses also the more broad-minded and liberal descriptions of American racial reality that by their empirical concentration upon a "minority" governed by the actions of powerful external forces sustains the reductive idea of a Black destiny dependent upon white initiative. The very term *minority* is called into existence by a "majority" culture, implicitly distinct and, by the fact of superior numbers, economic and political influence, and directive position in society, assuming the status of the normative civilization. What is true of the language of social scientific investigation is true as well of the putatively scientific thought of naturalistic literature. Through the syntax of its narrative techniques, it, too, depicts the leading characters of its fundamental plot as hapless subjects of alien necessity. Moving among these ways of encoding reality that have become traditional in the discourse of Black experience, *The Man Who Cried I Am* challenges their authority, first, by demystifying the claim to humanism that justifies white dominance in Western politics and literature and, second, by appropriating the form of the novel to a more accurate representation of perception and historical understanding than has normally been offered by either American historical or "problem" fiction. Portraying the action of his narrative in terms of the integration of Max Reddick's consciousness of memory's replotting social and personal experience along the axis of Harry Ames's account of the significance of King Alfred, Williams liberates his text from both American racial ideology and the narrative manner that in naturalism endorses such ideology. ⟨. . .⟩

This bleak and remarkable novel shows us that, to escape becoming victims of history, we must neither leave history unquestioned nor relate it as inevitable. Politics may be oppressive, but in the act of narration politics becomes subject to will and knowledge and inventive craft. Strictly speaking, of course, history is not a text, neither a master text such as the King Alfred Plan nor even a masterfully conceived novel such as *The Man Who Cried I Am*. Still history becomes accessible only through texts; it is the absent cause of fictions. To know history, then, we must act as we read and write, with the same creative force and imagination that produce narrative. That is the substantive truth uncovered in John A. Williams's thriller novel.

> John M. Reilly, "Thinking History in *The Man Who Cried I Am*," *Black American Literature Forum* 21, Nos. 1 & 2 (Spring–Summer 1987): 39–40

# ❖ *Bibliography*

*The Angry Ones*. 1960.

*Night Song*. 1961.

*The Angry Black* (editor). 1962, 1966 (as *Beyond the Angry Black*).

*Africa: Her History, Lands, and People*. 1962, 1965, 1969, 1973.

*Sissie*. 1963.

*The Protectors: The Heroic Story of the Narcotics Agents, Citizens, and Officials in Their Unending, Unsung Battles against Organized Crime in America and Abroad* (with Harry J. Anslinger). 1964.

*This Is My Country Too*. 1965.

*The Man Who Cried I Am*. 1967.

*Sons of Darkness, Sons of Light: A Novel of Some Probability*. 1969.

*The Most Native of Sons: A Biography of Richard Wright*. 1970.

*The King God Didn't Save: Reflections on the Life and Death of Martin Luther King, Jr.* 1970.

*Amistad: Writings on Black History and Culture* (editor; with Charles F. Harris). 1970–71. 2 vols.

*Captain Blackman*. 1972.

*Flashbacks: A Twenty-Year Diary of Article Writing*. 1973.

*Mothersill and the Foxes*. 1975.

*Minorities in the City*. 1975.

*The Junior Bachelor Society*. 1976.

*Yardbird No. 1* (editor). 1979.

*!Click Song*. 1982.

*Last Flight from Ambo Ber*. 1983.

*The Berhama Account.* 1985.

*The McGraw-Hill Introduction to Literature* (editor; with Gilbert H. Muller).
    1985.

*Jacob's Ladder.* 1987.

*Love.* 1988.

*If I Stop I'll Die: The Comedy and Tragedy of Richard Pryor* (with Dennis A.
    Williams). 1991.

*Bridges: Literature Across Cultures* (editor; with Gilbert H. Muller). 1994.

*Ways In: Approaches to Reading and Writing about Literature* (with Gilbert H.
    Muller). 1994.

⬚ ⬚ ⬚

# Frank Yerby
## *1916–1991*

FRANK GARVIN YERBY was born on September 5, 1916, in Augusta, Georgia, the son of a black father and a Scotch-Irish mother. He attended a private black school in Augusta, the Haines Institute, then entered Paine College, where he received a B.A. in English in 1937. The next year he received an M.A. from Fisk University in Nashville, Tennessee. In 1939 he began work on a Ph.D. at the University of Chicago, but left after less than a year for financial reasons. He worked briefly with the Federal Writers' Project in Chicago, meeting such black writers as Richard Wright and Arna Bontemps. After leaving Chicago he taught briefly at Florida A&M University in Tallahassee and at Southern University in Baton Rouge, Louisiana. He married Flora Williams in 1941; they had four children but would eventually divorce.

Yerby worked for the Ford Motor Company in Dearborn, Michigan, for three years (1941–44) as a laboratory technician; the next year he worked for Ranger (Fairchild) Aircraft in Jamaica, New York. Although Yerby had published a few short stories and poems in college and literary magazines, it was during the war that he began writing in earnest. The short story "Health Card," published in *Harper's Magazine* for May 1944, received the O. Henry Memorial Award for best first short story. This searing tale of the mistreatment of a black couple in the military was followed by several other short stories on the plight of black Americans in a racist society; but Yerby felt that restricting his writing to racial issues would limit his audience, so he set out to write a "costume" novel that might have wider appeal. The result was *The Foxes of Harrow*. Published in 1946 by the Dial Press (which issued nearly all his novels), it became an instant best-seller and was later made into the film *Foxes*, starring Rex Harrison and Maureen O'Hara.

Although Yerby admitted in an interview that "I set out to write the worst possible novel it was humanly possible to write and still get published but it sort of got hold of me, and about half way through, I started revising and improving it," he came to take pride in the writing of novels that merely "entertained" without addressing serious social or political issues. His thirty-three novels sold nearly sixty million copies, making him by far the most widely read black American writer in history. Many readers were not even aware that he was black. Several of his works have been adapted for film and television. Critics have found that racial and other serious messages nevertheless enter into his work, in the guise of outsiders who triumph over obstacles by their courage, strength, or cunning. Some novels do in fact deal in part with the oppression of minority races, and *The Dahomean* (1971) is a sympathetic story of an African tribe.

In 1952 Yerby moved to France. Three years later he made a visit to Spain, where he met a Spanish woman, Blanca Calle-Perez, whom he married in 1956; he lived in Madrid for the rest of his life. Frank Yerby died of heart failure on November 29, 1991. While reviewers and critics passed off most of his books as potboilers, black critics were divided over the merits of his work. Some criticized him for not addressing racial themes more seriously and systematically, while others praised him for writing "raceless" novels that broadened the subject-matter available for black writers beyond narrowly racial issues.

# ◈ Critical Extracts

**RICHARD MATCH**     ⟨*The Foxes of Harrow*⟩ is a good, old-fashioned, obese historical novel of the Old South that seems, more than once, to be haunted by the affluent ghost of Scarlett O'Hara. It is the story of Irish Stephen Fox—"tall, red-haired, with a face that looked like Lucifer's so soon after the fall that the angel-look was still on it"—who came back to New Orleans in 1825 and parlayed a pearl stickpin and a devilish way with cards into the greatest sugar fortune in Louisiana. ⟨. . .⟩

Frank Yerby, who won an O. Henry Memorial Award for a short story last year, is a former student at Fisk University. In this, his first novel, one might have hoped for the ideological intensity of, say, Howard Fast's *Freedom Road*, and, indeed, there are some sympathetic evidences of the Negro's deep resentment against slavery. Mr. Yerby has chosen, however, to concentrate on a conventional historical narrative of passionate amours and gentlemanly swordplay.

> Richard Match, "The Vulpine Master of Harrow," *New York Times Book Review*, 10 February 1946, p. 8

---

**HUGH M. GLOSTER**     Despite their popular appeal, *The Foxes of Harrow* and *The Vixens* do not establish Yerby as a first-rate novelist. The use of secondhand materials, which provoked one critic (James MacBride in the New York *Times Book Review* for May 4, 1947) to refer to *The Vixens* as a "grab-bag of stereopticons" that Yerby "shuffled between covers and labeled a novel," causes the reader to think that the young writer knows more about libraries than about life. Furthermore, the author's seeming lack of ideological conviction is somewhat unexpected in fiction treating the cross-currents of life and thought in nineteenth-century Louisiana. Yerby also has a flair for melodrama which impelled one reviewer (see *Time* for May 5, 1947) to classify both *The Foxes of Harrow* and *The Vixens* as "drugstore fiction." While the assignment of Yerby's first novel to this category is highly debatable, the criticism does point to an inclination which assumes sizable proportions in *The Vixens*. ⟨. . .⟩

Nevertheless, Yerby has assets as a writer. He shows intimate knowledge, gained through study and research, of his locale and its history. He exercises balance in handling inflammatory, controversial subjects. He has faculty in the use of words, especially pictorial and passionate ones, and the power to maintain interest from the beginning of a tale to its close. His chief contribution, however, has been to shake himself free of the shackles of race and to use the treasure-trove of American experience—rather than restrictively Negro experience—as his literary province. *The Foxes of Harrow* and *The Vixens*, along with Willard Motley's *Knock on Any Door*, signalize the emergence of Negro novelists from the circumscriptions of color and the power of these writers to treat competently not only various aspects of Negro experience but also the broader life of this country and the world.

> Hugh M. Gloster, "The Significance of Frank Yerby," *Crisis* 55, No. 1 (January 1948): 13

---

**HARVEY BREIT**     Every once in a while—not often, mind you—there appears on the literary horizon an author who, for one reason or another, can't help but produce best-selling novels. Frances Parkinson Keyes is one such. Frank Yerby is another. Now, take Frank Yerby: at the ripe age of not quite thirty-five, he has come up with his sixth novel, A *Woman Called Fancy*, and the chances are very good (as good, say, as Ray Robinson beating Jack LaMotta in a rematch) that it will be a thumping best seller, as were the five novels before it. Each of the five were book-club selections and each had a distribution of at least a million copies. *The Foxes of Harrow*, Mr. Yerby's first, went to over two million. ⟨. . .⟩

How did Mr. Yerby write a novel? "I've done a novel every year for six years," Mr. Yerby said. That meant, then, quite a tight regimen, didn't it? Mr. Yerby nodded. "I frequently write right around the clock," he said. "I work as much as eighteen hours a day. Not only that; I rewrite. I rewrote *Fancy* three times. And not only that: I do a lot of research. I read, read, read for my preliminary work. I've been spending as much as six hours a day in the library on background material for my new novel."

Mr. Yerby didn't exactly hesitate. He said, "My notes for a novel always outweigh in bulk the novel itself. Sometimes it's three times over." Well, this data struck an observer as all to the good; at least, one could feel, Mr. Yerby's novels weren't "quickies." It turned out that Mr. Yerby had pretty strong feelings on the entire matter of the relationship between writer and reader.

"I think the novelist," Mr. Yerby said, "has a professional obligation to please his reading public." At the age of twenty, when Mr. Yerby was writing poetry for the little magazines, was he writing for any other reason than that he had to? Or wasn't that it? Of course that was it. "Because a writer has a duty to his reader," Mr. Yerby said with honest passion, "it doesn't mean in any way that he has the right to write *down* to his reader. All the brows, high, middle and low, should be able to read his book, but for different reasons. The novelist has no right whatsoever to insult his public."

Harvey Breit, "Frank Yerby" (1951), *The Writer Observed* (Cleveland: World Publishing Co., 1956), pp. 195–96

---

**EDWARD J. FITZGERALD**      Ever a fast man with clichés, Frank Yerby has here ⟨in A *Woman Called Fancy*⟩ piled them on so fast and so thick that one might almost believe he is attempting to burlesque himself. His sixth assault on the best-seller lists is concerned with the tribulations and triumphs of Fancy Williamson, a good girl—poor as a churchmouse, pure as driven snow, honest as the day is long, and of a beauty that sets men's pulses racing. ⟨. . .⟩

It is customary to wonder what the strange quality is that causes so many millions of people to purchase Mr. Yerby's efforts. I cannot imagine, but I know they'll go for this one.

Edward J. Fitzgerald, [Review of A Woman Called Fancy], Saturday Review of Literature, 23 June 1951, p. 39

**NICK AARON FORD**     Frank Yerby's first literary recognition came nine years ago (1944) when his "Health Card" was awarded the O. Henry Memorial Prize of one hundred dollars for the best "first published short story" of the year. Already the twenty-eight-year-old author had behind him seventeen years of academic training, climaxed by the degree of Master of Arts, and a brief teaching career in two Negro colleges.

"Health Card" is a bitter story of America's rejection of the Negro as a dignified human being, as a person who has sensibilities that should be respected by his countrymen. It is bitter and pathetic, for it leaves the impression that there is no help for the intolerable situation. ⟨. . .⟩

Mr. Yerby has dedicated himself to the proposition that a novelist must not take sides in the controvesial, political, religious, or racial issues inherent in the material he uses. He even confides in a statement for public print that when he reads *Anna Karenina* he skips the political discussion concerning the peasant-land situation in Russia with which Tolstoy was passionately concerned. He says, "That sort of thing just isn't the novelist's job." He agrees that it is important for the novelist to know his character's emotional life, his emotional reaction to political ideas, but he asserts that what the political ideas themselves are should be a matter of indifference to the novelist. "The novelist hasn't any right," he insists, "to inflict on the public his private ideas on politics, religion or race. If he wants to preach he should go on the pulpit." ⟨. . .⟩

Now, all of this is not to say that Yerby is an inferior writer. He has rich imagination, a talent for vivid expression, ability to create pity and terror, and an understanding of the suffering of the poor and the oppressed. In short, he possesses the qualifications that could make of him a great novelist. But it appears that Yerby is satisfied with popularity without greatness. He says emphatically, "I think the novelist has a professional obligation to please his reading public."

Nick Aaron Ford, "Four Popular Negro Novelists," *Phylon* 15, No. 1 (First Quarter 1954): 37–38

---

**FRANK YERBY**       Inescapably, the costume novel belongs to what has been called escape literature. I have often wondered, with weary patience, why that term is used by critics as a dirty word. Considered coldly, what kind of fiction is not escapist? The route indicated by the novelist may differ markedly; but the destination is still the never-never land of the spirit, of imagination; and all the arrows point away from the here and now. Your writer guide may take you through the South Side of Chicago, down Los Angeles' Skid Row, rub your refined nostrils in the raw odors of realism; but you know, and he knows, that you don't read his opus if you live on the South Side, Skid Row, or the Bowery—or even if you happen to be a *clochard* sleeping in the cold and wet under one of the bridges of the Seine.

If he is honest, as he so seldom is, the novelist will admit that at best he is aiming for a carefully contrived, hypnotic suspension of his reader's sense of disbelief—not even for a real slice of life. Because, in life, people think of the proper response two hours, or two days, too late; things go wrong, not upon the respectable scale of tragedy, but on the slow, bumbling, painfully embarrassing, minuscule dimensions of inept, amateur farce. In life, conversation is an endless series of *non sequiturs*, of windy nonsense, or of just plain dull nonsense. And no realist would ever dare pinpoint on paper the most realistic of all life's attributes: the thundering, crashing boredom of the life of the average man.

The point of all this is, I suppose, that novels written with the deliberate intention to amuse or entertain have—or should have—a very real place in contemporary literature. It seems to me that people have the right to escape occasionally and temporarily from life's sprawling messiness, satisfy their hunger for neat patterns, retreat into a dreamlife where boy gets girl and it all comes out right in the end always. They need such escapes to help them endure the shapelessness of modern existence. It is only when they try to escape permanently that the trip out to Kansas and Karl Menninger's becomes indicated. I honestly believe that thumbing through an occasional detective yarn, science-fiction tale, or costume novel, is rather better preventive therapy than tranquilizers, for instance.

Frank Yerby, "How and Why I Write the Costume Novel," *Harper's Magazine* 219, No. 4 (October 1959): 149–50

---

**DARWIN T. TURNER**     Chiefly, of course, ⟨Yerby⟩ has attacked America, in particular the South. Until recent years this section of America has received literary glorification as a region of culture and gentility. The males reputedly were aristocratic, cultured, brave, and honorable. The females were gentle and chaste. Savagely, Yerby has ridiculed these myths. ⟨. . .⟩

Unlike a typical propagandist, however, Yerby has not restricted his attack to one group. He has also castigated Americans above the Maxon-Dixon line. In *Floodtide*, Morgan Brittany, a Northern emigrant, mouths platitudinous protests against slavery; soon, however, she gratifies her perverted lusts by beating her chained slaves. Most of the sadistic overseers, Yerby has alleged, were reared in the North. New Yorkers evidenced their bigotry when they slaughtered Negroes whom they blamed for the North's involvement in the Civil War. Northern businessmen exploited white laborers as shamefully as Southern planters had exploited slaves (*Pride's Castle*, 1949). During Reconstruction, carpetbaggers from the North ignobly amassed fortunes by preying upon the conquered people (*The Vixens*, 1947).

Yerby has not spared Negroes. Depicting cringing slaves who fawn upon their masters and betray their fellows, he has argued that the American slaves rarely rebelled because the traders wisely selected them predominantly from tribes made docile by centuries of bondage in Africa. In contrast, the slaves of Haiti, carelessly selected from proud and warlike tribes, overthrew their French masters. Furthermore, having been restricted to a childlike existence devoid of formal education, dignity, or opportunity to assume responsibility for their welfare, American slaves, when freed suddenly, could not govern themselves. Few, consequently, proved capable of governing wisely in the Southern legislatures.

Regardless of their wealth or talent, free Southern Negroes, he has argued, were excluded from society, denied dignity, and robbed even of the power to protect their women—those who acted like men were shot (*The Foxes of Harrow*). Yet, unwilling to identify themselves with slaves, they often compensated for their own humiliation by abusing darker-skinned Negroes

(*Captain Rebel*). Educated Northern Negroes doubted the educability of Southern Negroes and sometimes adjudged themselves inferior to less-educated white men (*Griffin's Way*). 〈. . .〉

Yerby is no misanthrope; he has heroes: Thomas Jefferson, who freed his slaves; George Washington, who led American revolutionists heroically despite his incompetence as a military tactician; Henri Christophe, who helped free Haiti from French authority. Moreover, Yerby has struggled to evolve a positive philosophy. Significantly, he has repudiated the patient goodness frequently held before Negroes as a desirable standard. Yerby persists in showing that men succeed and are extolled because they are smarter, stronger, bolder, and braver than other men. Sometimes, they act morally and honorably; more often they do not. But neither their contemporaries nor their descendants evaluate the morality of the successful, the heroes. The minority groups in Yerby's stories suffer because they are ignorant, weak, and cowardly. Foolishly, they beg for help from a deity, which, according to Yerby, if it exists, views mankind hostilely, indifferently, or contemptuously. Life has meaning only when man—frail and insignificant— sparkles as brightly as possible in his instant of eternity.

Darwin T. Turner, "Frank Yerby as Debunker," *Massachusetts Review* 9, No. 3 (Summer 1968): 572–76

---

**DARWIN T. TURNER**      Set in nineteenth century Africa, *The Dahomean* traces the life of Nyasanu, second son of a village chief, who rises to power as the governor (*gbonuga*) of a province, struggles to maintain political control over his territory and domestic control over a household of seven wives (two inherited from his father) and one concubine, but is finally betrayed and sold into slavery by a villainous half-brother and an equally villainous brother-in-law. A relatively simple plot for a book of almost 400 pages; an incredibly uncomplicated plot for Yerby fans accustomed to the mazes of a *Floodtide*, where villains, wives, friends, relatives, and various secondary characters all command individual subplots traced relentlessly until their adventures finally return them to the proximity of the protagonist. Not so, in *The Dahomean*. A major virtue of the work is that one can concentrate without distraction on the Black hero. 〈. . .〉

〈. . .〉 In Yerby's one previous novel about a Negro protagonist, the ancestral brainwashing so colored the protagonist's thought that his very act of affirming his identity and equality emphasized his distinction from white Americans and Europeans. In *The Dahomean*, however, no such contrast obtrudes. Almost casually Yerby shows that the Africans judge the whites to be ugly because their color resembles that of animals who have been skinned, their hair seems as bleached as dead grass, their lips are not sensuous, and their women have no hips. The intelligent African does not bother to translate his language carefully for Furtoos ⟨whites⟩, who are too ignorant to comprehend the subtle nuances. Nevertheless, Yerby makes no concerted effort to demonstrate the superiority of the Africans to the Europeans. He does not need to. As the people with power, his Africans determine the standards of excellence. According to those standards—African or "Black"— the Europeans are inferior. Simply accepting this as a fact, the Africans in Yerby's book do not need to protest their superiority continuously in the manner of some contemporary white and Black Americans who bellow about racial superiority in order to deafen themselves to murmurs of insecurity. People who have the power to control their destinies (as far as the indifferent Fates will permit) do not need continuously to prove or argue their equality or superiority to other tribes which lack the power to compete. I think it is to Frank Yerby's credit that he recognized this truth. By doing so, he not only gave psychological strength to his story, he also validated an inference which can be drawn from his earlier stories: despite his years of rearing in the American South and despite his contempt for slaves who accepted the doctrine of inferiority, Yerby himself has never believed all Africans to be racially inferior to any other people. At least, he has never believed this of the Ashanti, the Dahomeans, and the Auyos.

The story clearly supports Yerby's philosophy that worldly success is not determined by one's goodness and virtue—or, in this case, by racial purity and blood—but by strength and by the intelligence and ruthlessness to use that strength towards one's ends. This, Yerby would say, holds true whether one is talking about Black people or white people or yellow people or purple people.

Darwin T. Turner, [Review of *The Dahomean*], *Black World* 21, No. 4 (February 1972): 51, 84–85

---

**JACK B. MOORE**     As a racial statement, *A Woman Called Fancy* seems confused. Perhaps Yerby was only honestly desiring to match the confusion about the race issue that his generally liberal white Southern heroes display. Yerby makes painfully clear the racist attitude of one of his most sympathetic and otherwise right-minded characters, Wyche Weathers. Wyche explains "what I mean is I have black friends—like old Maude, for instance, who manage to like me in spite of the fact that my skin's the wrong color from their point of view. But I have to admit that blacks and whites can't really live together. Not now, not ever. A Negro is just too damned physically different from a white man. . . . But the main trouble is, that the Negro in the mass is actually inferior to the white man in the mass, theories be damned." The speech does not seem needed to establish Weathers' character, nor does it advance the plot, and it is difficult to see why Yerby included it since verisimilitude could have been achieved through other means. Perhaps he wanted to suggest the overt racism that the best kind of Southern white could maintain and in this way criticize white society. But the technique seems dubiously effective, especially since Weathers' analysis of the Negro's alleged inferiority is otherwise relatively perceptive and shows that he considers its basis in some ways cruelly environmental. "What do you think it does to a bright boy to know it would cost him his life if he ever reared upon his haunches and acted like a man?" Wyche says "Being bought and sold like mules did something to them . . . you don't ever call a black man 'mister.' Up to forty-five he's 'boy,' and after that he's Uncle. . . . Then when they rear up and act like the beasts we've made of them, we lynch them with a barbaric savagery that would disgrace a Sioux. I don't like it. . . . A man pulling off his cap and shuffling his feet, and getting off the sidewalk to let me pass doesn't make me feel good inside."

Jack B. Moore, "The Guilt of the Victim: Racial Themes in Some Frank Yerby Novels," *Journal of Popular Culture* 8, No. 4 (Spring 1975): 749

**MICHELE SLUNG**     Fifty million copies of his 29 novels have been sold worldwide, and the 30th, *Western*, is being published this month. His mother spanked him, he says, when he was a child because he was continually making up stories, but readers in a dozen languages have reason to be grateful her discipline didn't stick. "A writer who has no audience isn't much of a writer," says Georgia-born Frank Yerby, speaking from his home on the outskirts of Madrid, where he has lived since 1956. Part black, part Scotch-Irish, part American Indian, he explains his expatriation in a voice that still has a definite southern flavor: "I had one solution to the racial problems of the United States—I bought an airline ticket." But his flippancy is a mask for old wounds that must still smart, and three of his books have featured black protagonists. However, he rightly insists, you can't judge books by their color. ⟨. . .⟩

A typical Yerby plot seems to involve a strong man who has to choose between two women, and there usually are more-than-generous helpings of revenge, madness, suffering and violence. It's a formula he's mastered, and he believes he sells "because one has learned one's craft and does one's job." Of his own work, Yerby's personal favorites are those he says no one else likes. *An Odor of Sanctity* (1965) is one he names, as well as *The Dahomean* (1971) and *The Garfield Honor* (1961)—this last being, he claims, "an accurate western, with no Hollywood legend allowed to creep in." ⟨. . .⟩

His 31st novel, *Devilseed*, "about the most outrageous female since Moll Flanders," is already delivered to Dial, and Yerby is starting to think whether or not he will base his 32nd on the little-known St. Patrick's Brigade, "some 300 Irish-Americans who deserted to Mexico during the Mexican-American War." His staying power and his imagination are keeping pace, and he's well aware that while popularity and respect often diverge the former is hardly a curse. "Thackeray," he reminded "Book Report" drily, "didn't starve."

Michele Slung, "Book Report: Frank Yerby Keeps Them Coming," *Washington Post Book World*, 15 August 1982, p. 15

---

**PHYLLIS R. KLOTMAN**      In Yerby's novel ⟨*The Foxes of Harrow*⟩, Stephen Fox is a "Dublin guttersnipe," a handsome, less-than-honest gambler who is put off a riverboat by the captain in the middle of the Mississippi. Saved by an Irish ruffian, he lands in New Orleans and gambles his way to enough money to acquire a plantation after killing a quarrelsome German from whom he has won both slaves and land. He builds Harrow, the most magnificent plantation in Louisiana, on the backs of 1500 slaves and acquires the proudest, most beautiful Creole belle in New Orleans for his wife. Unlike other conventional heroes of historical romance, however, he discovers that his pristine, pure virgin is frigid. Their life together becomes a nightmare of frustration and missed opportunities. Their son, raised by parents (and slaves) who deny him nothing, becomes an indolent, cruel, never quite happy young man who is so committed to the slave system and its racist

assumptions that he becomes involved in its maintenance and spread to
the border states. The novel covers a forty-year period (1825–1865), from
the apogee to the nadir of Southern fortunes. Stephen Fox's fortunes wax
and wane as he conquers yet another Southern belle and a beautiful qua-
droon, buries his wife, and helps the South lose the Civil War. In the end
he is somewhat ignominiously given his freedom from prison by one of his
former slaves.

I suppose it is not so curious that the first thing Hollywood did was
reinstate the myth. Stephen Fox becomes the son of an Irish noblewoman
whom we see briefly in a flashback which serves as a prologue to the film.
Like Fielding's Tom Jones, Stephen is born on a great estate (Harrow—
hence the name of the plantation he builds), and like Tom he is also a
bastard child. His mother has him spirited away—to be raised by peasants—
and with a highly unorthodox childhood behind him, he eventually finds
his way to America. When we see him as a handsome, dapper rogue (minus
the Irish brogue he has in the novel), he is being ejected from a Mississippi
riverboat for being rather too sleight of hand at the gaming table. The film,
quick to establish dramatic conflict, places the aristocratic flower of the
South at the scene of Stephen's embarrassment: Odalie Arceneaux looks
on with disdain. The only symbol of his noble birth is a pearl stickpin which
he cherishes, but it is there throughout the film to remind us that Stephen's
rise to fortune and power is predictable because he comes of the best stock.
Yet despite the manipulated Hollywood "happy" ending, the film has in
fact shown the extent to which two willful people can go to injure each
other and thereby their child. At the end of the film the relationship
between Stephen and Odalie has been irrevocably tainted, their son is dead,
and Harrow is near destruction. All this bodes ill for the future we do not
see (the Civil War is still some years ahead). In addition, the film draws
some unorthodox parallels between the experiences of blacks and whites,
implying that slaves were human beings who had the capacity to love, feel
pain and loss, and even the courage to try to save their children from the
slave system.

    Phyllis R. Klotman, "A Harrowing Experience: Frank Yerby's First Novel to Film,"
CLA Journal 31, No. 2 (December 1987): 213–14

---

**JAMES L. HILL**    Even though Frank Yerby's novels incorporate a
modern realistic perspective, they are, nonetheless, modifications of the

conventional picaresque novel. Like the anti-romantic picaresque fiction of earlier centuries, Yerby's costume novels are implicitly satirical of the heroic ideal and contain two poles of interest—one, the protagonist and his adventures; the other, the manners of the society that the protagonist pillories. Adhering to the pattern of the picaro, Yerby's protagonists are alienated by circumstances of birth or their past; they seek to establish themselves in an alien culture; and they always expect to accomplish their goals. Usually, however, they find very little that is permanent; for, either failing to know or disregarding the traditions of the societies they enter, these protagonists find themselves enmeshed in a series of conflicts and paradoxes. ⟨. . .⟩

Another trait of the Yerby anti-hero is that he is sometimes a ruthless opportunist. Rejecting the circumstances of his past life, he enters an alien culture as an outcast, and in that culture, he becomes both victimizer and victim. This anti-hero is an ambivalent character who both identifies with and rebels against society, in the manner of the contemporary anti-heroes of modern fiction. Or, in the case of most of the anti-heroes in Yerby's short fiction, they are oppressed and denied a respectable status in society, and they remain victims of oppression. Characteristically, the picaresque anti-hero in Yerby's costume novels does not represnt any movement or cause in society; his primary concern is with his individual quest.

Like the prototypical Existentialist hero, the Yerby anti-hero pits himself against the hostile forces of his environment. In his pursuit of the goal which will give meaning to his life, he reveals in actuality a life which lacks any real substance. Yerby's protagonist, however, differs from the Existentialist hero. He does maintain a sense of purpose and knows exactly what he wants or does not want. Usually, his identification with society is the avenue to his realization of the goal he seeks; but at the same time, he rebels against the restrictive morality and mores of that society, often remaining a marginal man. In addition, his disappointment with the goal he achieves in society frequently proves a source of further alienation.

Unlike the conventional romance hero, the protagonist in Yerby's novels is not always patriotic or heroic. He often engages in perilous adventures, but he finds neither glory nor honor in them. Most Yerby protagonists, for example, express their disdain or hatred of war even though they fight heroically. Additionally, the Yerby anti-hero does not conform to any particular societal code. He is a visionary who, in his rise to success, victimizes all who stand between him and his goal; however, in the process of realizing his visions, he becomes himself a victim of society. He inherits the burden of the traditions of society and finds himself oscillating between tradition and individualism, alienation and opportunism, rebellion and acceptance. Constantly buffeted by fate in his pursuit of an elusive goal, he usually comes to accept in old age what he would have earlier refused. These distinct aspects of the characterization of the Yerby anti-heroic protagonist are recurrent in most of his novels. Essentially, they reveal the nature of the main genre pattern and the three patterns of characterization in his fiction: (1) mock-romance, (2) societal alienation, (3) amoral codes of behavior and (4) self-determined fate. In Yerby's fiction, some or all of these four distinct patterns constitute and illustrate his uses of the anti-heroic mode.

> James L. Hill, "The Anti-Heroic Hero in Frank Yerby's Historical Novels," *Perspectives of Black Popular Culture*, ed. Harry B. Shaw (Bowling Green, OH: Bowling Green State University Popular Press, 1990), pp. 146–47

# ▓ Bibliography

*The Foxes of Harrow.*. 1946.

*The Vixens.* 1947.

*The Golden Hawk.* 1948.

*Pride's Castle.* 1949.

*Floodtide.* 1950.

*A Woman Called Fancy.* 1951.

*The Saracen Blade.* 1952.

*The Devil's Laughter.* 1953.

*Benton's Row.* 1954.

*Bride of Liberty.* 1954.

*The Treasure of Pleasant Valley.* 1955.

*Captain Rebel.* 1956.

*Fairoaks.* 1957.

*The Serpent and the Staff.* 1958.

*Jarrett's Jade.* 1959.

*Gillian.* 1960.

*The Garfield Honor.* 1961.

*Griffin's Way.* 1962.

*The Old Gods Laugh: A Modern Romance.* 1964.

*An Odor of Sanctity: A Novel of Medieval Moorish Spain.* 1965.

*Goat Song: A Novel of Ancient Greece.* 1967.

*Judas, My Brother: The Story of the Thirteenth Disciple: An Historical Novel.* 1968.

*Speak Now: A Modern Novel.* 1969.

*The Dahomean: An Historican Novel.* 1971.

*The Girl from Storyville: A Victorian Novel.* 1972.

*The Voyage Unplanned.* 1974.

*Tobias and the Angel.* 1975.

*A Rose for Ana Maria.* 1976.

*Hail the Conquering Hero.* 1978.

*A Darkness at Ingraham's Crest: A Tale of the Slaveholding South.* 1979.

*Western: A Saga of the Great Plains.* 1982.

*Devilseed.* 1984.

*McKenzie's Hundred.* 1985.